A MARINE DIVE-BOMBER PILOT AT GUADALCANAL

I0895535

The SBD in a dive, drawn by Charles E. Showalter, author's rear-seat gunner.

A MARINE DIVE-BOMBER PILOT AT GUADALCANAL

Colonel
John Howard McEniry, Jr.
USMCR Ret.

THE UNIVERSITY OF
ALABAMA PRESS

Copyright © 1987 by
The University of Alabama Press
Tuscaloosa, Alabama 35487

ALL RIGHTS RESERVED

Manufactured in the United States of America

LIBRARY OF CONGRESS CATALOGING-IN-PUBLICATION DATA

McEniry, John Howard, Jr., 1917–
A marine dive-bomber pilot at Guadalcanal.

Bibliography: p. Includes index.
1. McEniry, John Howard, Jr., 1917– . 2. World War, 1939–1945—Aerial operations, American. 3. World War, 1939–1945—Campaigns—Solomon Islands—Guadalcanal Island. 4. World War, 1939–1945—Personal narratives, American. 5. United States Marine Corps—Biography. 6. Dive-bomber pilots—United States—Biography. 7. Guadalcanal Island (Solomon Islands)—History. I. Title.
D790.M333 1987 940.54'4973 86-16053

ISBN 0-8173-0330-8 (alk. paper)

DESIGNED BY LAURY A. EGAN

0-8173-1283-8 (pbk: alk. paper)

Dedicated to the memory of
Major Joseph Sailer, Jr.
AND
Second Lieutenant Charles E. Kollman

Maj. Joe Sailer, commanding officer of VMSB-132, shot down on December 7, 1942. He had the best record of any dive-bombing pilot in World War II and was credited with nine hits on ships in thirteen attacks. He was awarded the Navy Cross. (Official U.S. Marine Corps Photograph)

Charles E. Kollman, commanding officer of the Marine Air Reserve Training Detachment, Lincoln, Nebraska. As a second lieutenant, Kollman was presented a Japanese sword by General Vandegrift on December 9, 1942, for doing the most damage to the Japanese Navy. He was awarded the Navy Cross. (Official Photograph, U.S. Navy)

Contents

Acknowledgments

I started this book as a record of events with the thought that it would be of some interest to my grandchildren in their later years. It was originally begun about ten years ago when I was engaged in the active practice of law, but it soon became evident that it was too much of an undertaking, and I put it aside.

Later, health dictated that I retire from the law, and the initial shock of retirement was such that I knew I must do something to occupy myself or I would run both myself and my wife crazy. It then occurred to me to complete the book, and I had the typewriter I had used in law school cleaned and oiled and sat down to write. I had not used a typewriter since law school, and I was surprised at how quickly the keyboard came back to me.

After the manuscript was completed, I sent it to several friends for their comments and suggestions. They were all most helpful in recommending additions and deletions. I am particularly indebted to Ben Robertshaw, Hap Simpson, Russ Janson, Jug Herlihy, Tex Kelly, and John Stock for their help and to John Stock and Jug Herlihy for the stories which are a part of the book. The historical section of the Marine Corps furnished me with the appropriate squadron and group histories, which gave me the names of the ones who were on a particular flight. The sketch of the SBD in a dive was drawn by Charles E. Showalter, my rear-seat gunner. He has acquired much recognition in the art field since his retirement from the Corps.

A MARINE DIVE-BOMBER PILOT AT GUADALCANAL

Introduction

This account is written for my own enjoyment and for that of some of my friends with whom I flew and laughed on Guadalcanal. Someone should record the trials and tribulations of these past events. These are my recollections. I do not guarantee accuracy on the names of the ones involved in all cases, but my memory is backed up in some instances with diaries kept in violation of the rules by Archie (Hap) Simpson, Russ Janson, and myself, the squadron war diary, and the notes of others. Every person who is named is a close personal friend, and each will quickly recognize names they do not know as those which have been changed "to protect the innocent." Many of the details of this part of our lives are undoubtedly submerged in our subconscious. This record may bring these events to the surface, cause a warm smile, and even induce interested questions from our children.

A brief background of the writer might be in order to understand better some of my attitudes and perspectives. I was born in Bessemer, a small, industrial town in Alabama. My father was a lawyer and during the Republican administration was the postmaster. When Roosevelt was elected in 1932, he returned to the practice of law, and it was necessary for my mother to go to work.

My early years were typical of a boy growing up during the depression in such a town. When I was sixteen years old and about to be a senior in high school, I went to Europe with a cousin seventeen years of age, a freshman in college. Together we worked our way on a freighter out of Mobile and spent most of the summer going around Germany and the Low Countries. When I came home I was much in demand on the local lecture circuit: the surrounding high schools, civic clubs, and the like, because our trip was quite unusual at that time. Most of the credit for the adventure belonged to my cousin, who later achieved a prominent place in higher education, serving finally as head of the Southern Association of Colleges and Secondary Schools.

We had left Mobile with $100 each in a handmade chamois-skin money bag sewn onto elastic belts made by our mothers. Once on the ship, we found that in port we would have no duties. The ship was to dock first in Bremen, then go to Hamburg to finish unloading, and finally to Antwerp, Belgium, to load for the return voyage.

The food and living conditions were simply awful. We ate only after the crew had eaten and were fed only the leftovers. We were not a part of the crew but were called "workaways." At sea, we had regular duties but were paid nothing. We decided that going home any other way was better than the way we came, and that if we were stranded the American Consul would have to arrange passage home. (I wonder whether this was so.) After we had been in Bremen for a day or so we decided to try to get to Moscow. The United States had only recently recognized the Soviet government. We packed our bags and left the ship to get a train for as far as our money would permit.

The streetcar we caught to go to the railroad station was going the wrong way, and we ended up in the best residential section of Bremen. We got off to await a trolley in the other direction, and while we were waiting a man by the name of Frederick Kreiger came along in a chauffeur-driven limousine. Our appearance was so unusual that he stopped and asked if he could help. We explained to him that we were waiting for the streetcar and he offered to take us downtown. He was head of the Bremen Cotton Exchange, the second largest in the world, had been in the United States several times, and spoke perfect English. As is natural with young people, we told him of our plans. His reaction was like that of any parent, and he pointed out that our parents would be ashamed of us.

He took us to his office and called in his man in charge of transportation, who arranged a trip around Germany:

from Bremen to Leipzig to Dresden to Berlin and then to Hamburg, back to the ship. He arranged our tickets at 60 percent off on some special fare and gave us the names of good but cheap hotels in each city. He then took us to the best hotel in town and paid for us to have the finest accommodations in the hotel. It was a suite of rooms. I have never stayed in as fine quarters since.

He then took us on a tour of Bremen. Hitler had only recently come to power and we were somewhat familiar with the Jewish problem. When we asked him about it, he explained that the Jews were only a small proportion of the German population but controlled 80 percent of the wealth and most of the government offices, and that the only thing Hitler was doing was redistributing the wealth and power. He showed us one large downtown building after another and said they were owned by Jews and that they would be compensated for them. He went over the Treaty of Versailles and told us how it had ruined Germany and that some corrections were necessary under the circumstances. In short he made a real impression on two children at an impressionable age.

Later while in college I took a major in history and political science. Dr. Howe, head of the department, arranged for a guest lecturer, Prince Alfred Lowenstein. The year was about 1939, and Europe was at war. The Prince told us of Hitler's excesses. I didn't believe a word of it and asked him whether he had heard of Frederick Kreiger. He said he knew him and respected his views. I told him of my experience with him and that his views conflicted with those of Mr. Kreiger. The Prince asked me whether I had heard from him. I had not. He said he was in a concentration camp. I really did not believe him.

The high school football coach had prevailed on me to stay over in high school for an additional year on the promise of a football scholarship, but I suffered a broken ankle before the first game of the season. He was as good as his word, however, and obtained a scholarship for me at Birmingham-Southern College, a small Methodist school. Looking for bigger things, I turned it down. I graduated as salutatorian of class in midterm and went to the University of Alabama with the intention of earning the scholarship there. My father had told me that he could pay for only my first year at college and that I would have to look for a way to assist with my education. Watching others on the football team, seeing the time and effort required and the harassment of freshman players convinced me that there was an easier way to make my way through school, and I changed my mind. I was able through working during the school year and in some of the summers to go to the University and live a normal student life. Things improved financially, and my family was able to help each year.

Since I had lost a year and entered college at midterm, I took a maximum load as an undergraduate and supplemented it with correspondence courses at home in the summer to make up the one semester I had missed. In college I was president of Jasons, a local honor society, vice-president of ODK, and president of my social fraternity during my junior year. My grades were a comfortable B+ average though my father was quite put out with me that I did not make Phi Beta Kappa. When he talked to me about its value after college, I maintained, typically, that leadership was more important. He insisted, without success, that I should aim for both leadership and academic excellence.

After completing the three years of undergraduate studies, I entered law school in the fall of 1939. At that time it was possible to obtain a B.A. degree after one year in law school following three years of undergraduate work and with two more years in law school get a law degree.

During the summers I was able to work in the ore mines at home for the magnificent sum of fifty-four cents an hour. This amounted to about $100 per month. Most of the miners were maintaining families on these wages. I felt fortunate to get such a fine job and would have been glad to work for half that amount. One of the miners asked me if they were going to save the job for me when I finished school.

During this time, my roommate and I enrolled in the Civilian Pilot Training Program and learned to fly. This was a forerunner of the present government-sponsored programs. All the expenses were paid by the government but as students we were paid nothing. At the end of my first year, I had obtained my private pilot's license. The next year we took an advanced course in acrobatic flying. Although flying was fun, I had no idea of ever using it later in life.

The Draft Act was passed in 1940, and in the fall of that year the numbers were pulled from the fish bowl to determine the order of going in. My number was the first to go from Bessemer. I was in my senior year in law school. The rules provided no deferment for college students except for those in their senior year. Since I had my B.A., I did not qualify, but I was able to convince the local draft board to defer me to the following July. At that time the draft was for one year, and it was my plan to spend my year as a private, come out, and practice law in Bessemer with my father and uncle.

During this final year the Governor of Alabama, Frank Dixon, came to the law school and made a patriotic speech. He had been a pilot in World War I and had lost his leg in an airplane accident. He took his walking cane and hit his artificial leg and said something to the effect that we should all be willing to sacrifice our lives for the country if it were necessary. We were not at war. I thought it was a ridiculous statement.

As the year went on, the draft was extended for a two-year period, and I decided that I should look to the possibility of getting a commission. In the spring of 1941, just before graduation, a Marine officer had come to the campus to recruit for the Marine officer training program. I applied but was not accepted because the program was for those who were to receive their undergraduate degrees in May. Since I already had my B.A., and was to get my LL.B.

in May, I was not eligible. It was my first encounter with Marine Corps red tape.

On the day I was taking my last examination, my roommate of the year before (who had graduated and was practicing law in a small South Alabama town) came by, found me, took my examination paper to the professor, and came back and said I had passed so he turned in the paper. (I had completed only seven of the ten questions, and I presumed the paper would be graded on a scale. We both knew the professor well. He was not much older than we, and his younger brother was a fraternity brother. It was a simple one-hour course and most of the students made an A on it. When the grade came back a D—the only D I had ever made—I went to the teacher. He asked what I expected when I had answered only seven of the ten problems.)

My roommate suggested that we go to Atlanta and join the "Marine Air Force." He was about to be drafted also. We went to Atlanta but found that the Marines were no longer recruiting aviation cadets. We would have to join the Navy as cadets and be selected for the Marine Corps at the proper time.

★ 1 ★

Background

I was ordered to flight training on July 1, 1941, and after some initial ground school instruction at an elimination base in Atlanta, I went to Pensacola on August 1. There were about 100 cadets in my flight class, all of whom had taken the Civilian Pilot Training Courses. Because of our past flying we began at an advanced stage of the training program, but the Navy training was so different from civilian flying that I almost washed out before I caught on to the Navy way. In civilian flying, safety was paramount. Not so with the Navy. I was almost a month behind my class before light finally dawned. From then on I had no problems. The acrobatic course I had taken put me ahead of the instructor in this phase, but when he flew through two outside loops, a particularly dangerous and difficult maneuver, in the N3N training plane, I gave up following what he was doing.

I had done well in military subjects and in the extensive ground school. I was number one in my class and was the cadet battalion commander. The Marine Corps was allowed to select 10 percent of each class. Since the word had come down that the Navy would assign all of our class as observation pilots on cruisers and battleships and therefore we would fly the slow observation planes, almost all of us applied for the Marines. Both my roommate and I applied and were accepted. This meant that we would go to the Naval Air Station at Miami for our final training in either fighters or dive-bombers. Because of my grades, I was able to take my choice. Rumor had it that the Marines at Quantico were getting A-20s, a hot new twin-engine bomber with only one pilot. I chose dive-bombers, thinking it would lead to the A-20s. Marines, however, were never given the A-20s. My roommate, who chose fighters, was subsequently killed while instructing after his tour of duty at Guadalcanal.

I completed flight school in March 1942 and was ordered to Quantico along with seven other newly commissioned second lieutenants for the ostensible purpose of attending communication school. The real purpose was to keep the Navy from making flight instructors of us. We showed up quite unexpectedly at Marine Corps Air Station (MCAS) Quantico and the powers that be really had nothing for us to do. They had only one SNJ (training plane) which we were not allowed to fly, and two outmoded planes, 1928 variety, to fly for flight pay, an FF-2 and an O3U.

When we were at Quantico, the people were far too busy to waste their time doing much with these second lieutenants, and except for an occasional school we were free to do almost anything we wanted to do. Our instructor was an old warrant officer who gave us only a brief introduction to the handling of classified materials. While we had been cadets in flight school at Miami an English pilot had told us about radar and how it operated. On leave, I had told my family in great detail all about this wonderful device that the English had. Then one night at Quantico, we were taken to a guarded room and given a very brief description of radar and subsequently escorted by guards with rifles to a very secret, darkened room and shown a radar screen. We were cautioned not to mention the word *radar* or talk even to each other about it. Having already told my parents of this wonderful new device in much detail, I frantically wrote to them and without using the word told them never to mention the thing that the English pilot had told me in flight school.

Quantico was a delightful place to be. We each bought six sets of white uniforms and ate our evening meals at the officers' club. While there, a number of the World War I pilots came back on active duty for training as Marine Air Group intelligence officers, group adjutants, and other similar ground jobs. They were an interesting group of men. We all took them flying in our back seats and found that they could fly the planes as well as we. For some of them it was their first time to fly since France. A number of Royal Canadian Air Force pilots also came to Quantico for indoctrination into the Marine Corps. These were all American citizens who for some reason or other (mainly the lack of educational requirements) had not been able to get into the Army or Navy flight training programs but were allowed to come in after our entry into the war. Some of them had wanted to get into the war before we entered and had joined for that reason. Most were barnstorming pilots and were real characters. One of them on a flight with me flew under the bridge across the Potomac outside of Washington, a maneuver strictly against all of the rules. I waited with bated breath to see if I was reported. I was not, but I never again let another one get his hands on the controls. One of the group, Don Aldridge, became quite well known as a fighter pilot at Guadalcanal, shooting down twenty planes, the fifth highest number in the Marine Corps.

During the latter part of June, six of us were to be ordered to the west coast for duty. We all knew that this meant further shipment overseas. All eight of us wanted to go. The remaining two were to be sent, one to Saint Thomas in the Virgin Islands and the other to the newly built Marine Corps Air Station at Cherry Point, North Carolina. Since all of us wanted combat duty, we had to draw lots to see who would get the duty with the First Wing. I'll never forget my relief when I drew the slip with First Wing on it. I still have the slip in my wallet. Both of the ones who did not get to go to the west coast were killed in operational accidents shortly after arriving at their new duty stations. On July 1, I was ordered to the First Marine Aircraft Wing at the Naval Air Station, San Diego, for duty. I had seven days leave en route.

When the time came for me to leave home, Dad took me to the train in Birmingham. I remember that I was surprised my mother did not go with us but said she would be at the station in Bessemer to wave as the train went through. I later realized that she was afraid she would make it hard for me if she broke down. To me, it was the great adventure.

The trip to San Diego was uneventful. Upon arrival and after going through a checking-in procedure which was always a nuisance, I was assigned to Advanced Carrier Training Group (ACTG). At that time most of the Marine pilots on the west coast had been sent overseas to Midway for the battle there or to Samoa to Marine Air Group (MAG) 13. There were very few Marine units at the Naval Air Station and those that were there had only skeleton manning. Here, Andy Jackson and I, who had been together in flight school and at Quantico, were again brought back together and I first met Felix ("Cisco") Cecot. The three of us were assigned to room together in the BOQ with a Navy pilot who had been at Pearl Harbor at the time of the attack. We learned from him—for the first time—of the real extent of the damage there.

Most of the newly commissioned Marines at the Naval Air Station were in ACTG, were attached to the First Marine Aircraft Wing (MAW), and had to stand inspection on Saturday mornings. At first inspection I was decked out in my uniform with the pre-Pearl Harbor ribbon and the sharpshooter medal I had won at Quantico. Next to me was an old, grizzled warrant officer with no decorations. When Gen. Lewis G. Merritt, the inspecting officer, came by, he asked him whether he rated any decorations and told him that at inspection he was expected to be in uniform with all of his ribbons. I thought that surely he knew he should be in uniform. The next Saturday at inspection I saw this same man again. He had more ribbons than I have ever seen, topped off with a Congressional Medal of Honor. He was Mike Widorcik. He had received his Congressional Medal as a private in World War I in France. Mike was the ordnance officer of Marine Air Group 11 and later I was privileged to get to know him. No one could have been nicer to a real "boot" than Mike. He introduced me to the "old Marine Corps" and told me how he had become a pilot. In the 1920s he was Capt. Roy Geiger's (later lieutenant general) plane captain. One of the pilots resigned and Geiger asked Mike whether he wanted to fly. When he said yes, he was told to have one of the lieutenants teach him. I am not sure whether he ever went to formal flight training or not. As the group ordnance officer, he saw to it that I was issued a 45-caliber pistol. I was now ready for war.

The training in ACTG was excellent but wild. Most of the assigned pilots were Navy ensigns just out of flight school and for the first time not under the strict supervision to which we had become accustomed. It was the only time I ever did acrobatics in formation and with people I did not know. One of the results was that more people were killed there than in combat. Each Sunday morning the station held a memorial service for those killed in ACTG the week before. There were about one hundred students in ACTG and services for five or six pilots were held each Sunday. But one did learn to fly an airplane. The dive-bombing training was outstanding. Field carrier landings taught us to handle a plane.

Freddie Gross had been with me at Quantico and we were in the same flight in ACTG. In a tail chase, Freddie pulled the wings off an SNJ (trainer) and the plane went straight down. I don't know how, but I was selected to escort his body home to Lonoke, Arkansas. As you would expect, Lonoke was a wide place in the road. I found another lieutenant in ACTG from another small town nearby and convinced him it was an opportunity to go home. I then went to the wing headquarters to tell them of my brilliant suggestion. Maj. Ed Pugh was the wing adjutant. I explained to him the benefits that would result from changing the orders, and for the first time in my short career, he stood me at attention and for about ten minutes carefully explained to me that the Marine Corps was not interested in any plans of second lieutenants; that our function was to say "Yes, sir," and that only. He ended by telling me that he was personally interested in how I performed this duty, and that if I did not perform to the level expected of a Marine officer, he would preside at my court martial.

Presuming that most readers have never had the dubious privilege of serving as an escort for a body, I will give a first-hand account of some of the trials and tribulations. I was met at the railroad station in San Diego and given the casket, together with a first-class ticket for the body to its destination. It being wartime, trains were so crowded that finding space to sit was sometimes a problem. All trains from San Diego go first to Los Angeles. When the body and I arrived there, I went to the baggage car to see that it was put on the right train, one going to Little Rock through Tucumcari, New Mexico, the "Route of the Rockets." Waiting by the baggage car, I saw an employee of the railroad come and put the casket into another baggage car. I asked where the car was going and was told that this car was headed for San Francisco. I told the trainman that the body was on the wrong train. Only because I was insistent, he checked and the error was corrected. Each time the train stopped thereafter, I went to the baggage car and, mindful of Major Pugh's interest in me, stood by until the train was ready to go. The conductor and I became good friends. He let me sleep in unoccupied beds en route, being careful to wake me before each stop while assuring me that it was not necessary for me to be so attentive to my assignment.

Three or four days later we arrived in Lonoke. Mrs. Gross very naturally wanted to see her son one more time. I explained to the funeral director the circumstances of Freddie's death, but she was insistent. I was saved only when one of the kinsmen who was a pilot in the Army came home for the funeral and I explained to him what had happened to Freddie. He handled the problem for me.

An escort must make, as a part of his duties, whatever burial arrangements the family wants. Mr. and Mrs. Gross asked me to please arrange a military funeral. Since Lonoke was about fifty miles east of Little Rock, I called the recruiting officer at Little Rock for help but received none. The funeral director suggested I contact an Army detachment at a nearby plant that manufactured artillery shells. He lent me a car and I drove to the plant with little hope of success, but the master sergeant in charge of the detachment there calmed my fears. He had completed a tour of duty at Arlington National Cemetery, and he and his detail put on the best military funeral you could imagine. The recruiting officer came to the funeral, was properly impressed, and did arrange my trip back to San Diego.

During the first part of October, when we were about to complete ACTG, Jackson, Cecot, and I were transferred to VMSB-132. ("VMSB" means "Heavier than Air Marine Scout Bomber.") I suppose we were among the last to join the squadron, though most of the others had only very recently joined. Robert E. "Tex" Kelly and Jack "Sperz" Sperzel had been members of the squadron for some time. I remember that I had only one flight with the squadron before we were told to go aboard the SS "MUMU," the code name for the *Lurline*, flagship of the Matson Line. There were 28 pilots, a doctor, engineering officer, adjutant, supply officer, an intelligence officer, and 243 men. All of the pilots were recently out of flight school except Maj. Joe Sailer, our commanding officer. Most of the officers and all of the enlisted men were complete strangers to me and to each other. The same was true of most of the others. Charlie Kollman, Russ Janson, and Wayne Gentry had finished ACTG in the flight just ahead of mine and were therefore friends but the majority of us had not known any of the others. Most of my flight classmates from flight school had been sent either to instructors school or overseas to Midway or to Samoa. We had our first chance to get to know each other on the ship on the way over.

★ 2 ★

The Military Situation, 1942

In the spring of 1942 the war did not go well for the United States. The Japanese had taken Wake, overrun the Philippines, Singapore, Malaya, Indonesia, and Burma, and were moving rapidly toward Australia. They had not lost a battle, and had taken each objective with little effort. They effectively controlled everything north of New Guinea and Samoa and west of Midway. America was fighting a defensive war and was not doing a very good job, but these defeats were not what had been expected. In flight school we were led to believe that the American Navy was so far superior to the Japanese that any war would be over in short order. One of my reactions to the news of Pearl Harbor was that the war would be over before I could finish flight school (a matter of about three months) and get to the Pacific.

In June, the Battle of Midway was joined, resulting in a resounding victory for our side, strictly because we were reading the Emperor's mail. Some of the brainy ones of the Navy had broken the Japanese codes. In this battle the Navy was able to sink four enemy carriers, with the resultant loss of a great number of highly trained pilots and other aviation personnel. The part of Marine aviation in this encounter was anything but spectacular. While a Marine dive-bomber and a fighter squadron were stationed on Midway, they were poorly equipped and most of the pilots were right out of flight school. The "Brewster Buffalo" (F2A), which most of the fighter pilots flew, had never been in combat and was never used again in combat. The pilots who flew them and were lucky enough to get back reported that the Zeros could fly loops around them when the F2As were at full throttle. Only two fighter planes were able to fly after they engaged the Japanese on the way in for the bombing raid. More than half of the fighter pilots were killed. The dive-bombers were worse off, if possible. Either they had SB2Us, so old that they had a fabric-covered fuselage, or they were equipped with the new SBD (new to them at that time). None of the pilots had ever flown them and had to glide-bomb rather than dive-bomb. Glide-bombing is not conducive to long life. In spite of all these problems, the Navy won the battle of Midway in a big, big way.

While the loss at Midway was discouraging to the Japanese, they did not see it as a stopping point but sent the troops which were to take and occupy Midway to New Guinea. In the spring of 1942, the Japanese high command had decided that they should take some measures to isolate Australia and in May had easily taken Tulagi, the British capital of the Solomon Islands. The government of the Solomon Islands, hearing that they were coming, evacuated a few days before their arrival. Some of the Australians who managed the coconut plantation for Lever Brothers or for Philip Burns took to the jungle, and they and the natives were later invaluable as "coastwatchers" who could keep us informed about Japanese movements and act as rescue units for pilots who, for whatever reason, were not able to return to base.

In March, the Navy had occupied the islands of Espiritu Santo and Vila in the New Hebrides group about 550 miles southeast of the Solomons. An airfield was constructed at Vila and shortly thereafter one was built at Espiritu Santo. Espiritu was a clean, beautiful island which served as our rest camp and the field where we reorganized after each of our tours in combat.

★ 3 ★

Dive-bombing Planes and Tactics

The SBD aircraft that we flew was a dive-bomber manufactured by the Douglas Aircraft Company, which had taken over the Northrop Aircraft Company. Northrop had won a contract to build a dive-bomber for the Navy in 1936. The BT, predecessor of the SBD, was a particularly unstable aircraft, and its use on carriers was unsatisfactory. When Douglas took over the contract in 1939, it redesigned the BT and it was redesignated as the SBD. Many of us flew our dive-bombing training hops at flight school in the old BTs. They leaked oil so badly that we were given a rag on the flight line for use in the air so that we could wipe the oil off the windshield in order to see.

The SBD came through several modifications down to the SBD-3, the aircraft which we flew to Guadalcanal. All of the planes at Guadalcanal were SBD-3s except one, which somehow was an SBD-2. The major difference between an SBD-3 and a 2 was in the hydraulic system. On the 2, it was necessary to slow down in order for the dive brakes to open, whereas in the 3s the dive brakes would open at any speed. This characteristic was of little consequence until you were into an attack where the antiaircraft fire was heavy and the approach was, of necessity, made at a relatively high speed. On those occasions, whoever had the 2 always finished his dive first since his dive brakes would not fully open and he went, as a consequence, much faster in the dive than anyone else. Somebody must have

An SBD over Guadalcanal in 1943. The bomb load can be seen on the bottom of the plane.

cracked up or been shot down in the 2, because it just disappeared after we had been there for two or three weeks.

The SBD-3 had a wingspan of 41 feet, a length of 32 feet, and a Wright R. 1820 engine with 1,000 horsepower. It had a cruising speed of about 140 knots and a climbing speed of 120 knots at about 200 feet per minute when carrying a 1,000-pound bomb. In a 70 degree dive with the dive brakes open, it had a terminal velocity of 240 knots. In a dive from about 12,000 feet, it took about 25 to 30 seconds to reach the release point of 1,500 feet. Upon occasion this seemed a lifetime but it gave time for any corrections made necessary by the wind and/or the movement of any target.

After we had had an opportunity to practice after our first tour of duty at Guadalcanal, most of us could hit within a fifty-foot circle at least half of the time, and were disappointed if all of our bombs did not fall within the one-hundred-foot circle. Strong winds and a fast-moving target such as a destroyer could have a disastrous effect on accuracy. As an example, during the minute when we were in the high-speed approach and the dive, a destroyer could execute a 180 degree turn, which made diving most difficult and diminished the chances for a hit. It must be remembered that during the time when we had the greatest opportunity to attack shipping, we were far from well trained. None of us, to my knowledge, had previously made a dive-bombing run with a real bomb.

The training of the squadron was the best that could be had under the circumstances but left much to be desired. Charlie Kollman, Russ Janson, and Wayne Gentry had each had the opportunity to finish ACTG, which would have given them a total of about 250 to 275 hours of flying with about 35 hours in an SBD. Herlihy, Cecot, Jackson, and I had completed the dive-bombing phase of ACTG and probably had about 25 hours of time in the SBD. The rest of the squadron, with the exception of Major Sailer, had had less time. Some of the pilots had had only a checkout flight in the aircraft. None of us had ever fired the machine guns on the SBD. None of us had ever dropped a live bomb. None of us had ever flown the plane at night. None of us had ever flown the plane on instruments.

As an example, one of the pilots, who will be nameless, came to me after we had been at Guadalcanal for some time and asked me to go over with him how to fire the two 50-caliber machine guns which were fired by the pilot forward through the propeller. He told me he had never been able to get his guns to fire and that ordnance had reported they were in working order each time. We went to one of the planes, and I asked him to show me what he did. He showed me how he charged both of the guns, turned on the gun switches, and then pulled the trigger, which was on the stick. That was all he knew. He did not understand that in order for the guns to fire it was necessary for the master arming switch to be turned on.

Another pilot asked me to check him on the bomb release, because he had brought back his bomb on several occasions, and the ordnance section had reported the plane to be okay. The SBD had a center rack and two wing racks for bombs. In the cockpit there was a bomb release handle with three slots. The slots on the outside would release only the bombs on the wing racks, but the center slot would release all of the racks including the center one. We seldom flew with anything on the wing racks, but we had a depth charge or a 500-pound or 1,000-pound bomb in the center. In some cases the ordnance man, after hanging the bomb on the center, would move the release handle to the wing rack so that the bomb would not be released in error. This pilot had flown the mission, taken the risks, and brought the bomb back without understanding the release mechanism. There were no handbooks on the SBD at Guadalcanal. I would be surprised if many of the planes even had their log books or engine logs.

The squadron which we were to relieve, VMSB-141, had come to the Canal in October and on the thirteenth, their commanding officer, executive officer, and flight officer, together with several of the pilots, were killed in a shelling. With all of their senior officers killed, they were like lost sheep, and they continued to suffer many losses. Our squadron was sent hurriedly without adequate training to replace them.

The formation flown by the SBDs was the usual three-plane sections, with the second section being flown up and to the right or left as the flight leader desired. If enemy fighters were encountered or were expected, the second section would move under and a little to the rear for protection and maneuverability. Each plane's rear-seat gunner had twin 30-caliber machine guns on a ring that gave the gunner a range of 180 degrees from side to side. The rear seat also pivoted upward so that he could cover from either side and up and down to some degree. Thus, in a formation of six planes, there were twelve guns that could conceivably be brought to bear on a fighter making a run from the rear. This was a good protection. I cannot remember a single plane being shot down while we were in this formation. Obviously, it was impossible to make a dive-bombing attack in this formation. On the *Lurline* on the way over, squadron tactics were discussed. There were three standard methods of entering a dive-bombing attack. If there were enemy fighters, the purpose was to stay together as long as we could, everyone getting into the bombing run as quickly as possible and effecting the rendezvous as quickly as possible after the attack. In one of the methods, the flight leader went into a gentle turn and then, at the proper time, waggled his wings as the standard attack signal. He then pulled up and over his inside wingman. The wingman toward whom the attack was made would then dive, followed by the wingman on the outside in the turn. The second section followed the same procedure. The advantages of this method were that the formation stayed together to the last possible moment, and each plane was in a slightly different angle for the antiaircraft gunners so that they had to make some adjustment. The disadvantage was that the wingmen and the following section leader were not able to see the target until they started into the dive, since flying in this formation required concentration on the flight leader.

If no enemy fighters were present, a second method might be used. The second section was put into an echelon away from the target, a gentle turn was made toward the target, and then it followed the same method of approach into the dive. The third method, by far the most satisfactory, put all planes into the echelon away from the target. In this formation all planes had more visibility, and the number of planes could be divided should there be more than one target. With ships there usually were ample targets.

Rendezvous was always made in the direction of the turn leading into the dive, unless it was prebriefed otherwise for some particular reason. The flight leader slowed his plane as soon as he was out of the range of antiaircraft fire, and the other planes remained at full throttle until rendezvous. The flight leader made a gentle 180 degree turn as soon as possible, and the other planes who had not joined up would cut inside the turn to get together at the earliest moment. Most rendezvous were accomplished immediately outside of the antiaircraft range because this was the favorite place for enemy fighters.

If the weather was good, we approached the target at about 12,000 to 13,000 feet. The throttle setting of the flight leader was such that the last man was able to keep up without undue trouble and make a fast let-down through antiaircraft fire to about 11,000 feet, when he would hope to be at about the pushover point. The flight leader would waggle his wings, pull up slightly, and drop the nose of the plane straight down, at which time he opened his dive brakes and started his run. The actual dive-bombing run was a series of small (one hoped) corrections for the speed of the target, the wind direction, and the torque of the plane. If the flight leader had misfigured his point of entry, it was necessary to correct on the way down—either steepening the dive, shallowing it, or making a correction to the right or the left. When the dive brakes first opened, there was a considerable slowing of the plane. The speed in the dive then increased until terminal velocity was attained. These speed changes caused corrections to be necessary for the directional stability of the plane—corrections made by changing the trim tabs on the rudder. The sight used for aiming was a three-power telescope placed above the instrument panel. If your plane was skidding, the sight was not then on the flight path and your bomb would not hit where your sight indicated. One degree of skid at a 1,500-foot release would throw the bomb about 28 feet. A destroyer was approximately 30 feet wide so that if you were in a skid you would not get even a near-miss.

In the dive-bombing run, until you reached about 4,000 to 5,000 feet, you were sighting with the nose of the plane and trying to correct for skid and reach an attitude so that your plane was straight up and down. In this attitude your flight tract was 70 degrees because of the lift on the wings. At this height the plane had reached its terminal velocity or near to it so that only small adjustments were necessary for the change in speed. Wind and target movement were the important factors. Now the pilot leaned forward and looked at the target through the telescopic sight, which had mil rings to assist in final allowances for wind, target movement, and degree of dive. When you felt that you were nearing the release altitude, it was necessary to take your eye off the sight, check your altimeter to determine your height, and put your eye back on the sight for final corrections.

The bomb fuses were armed by a small propeller on the front of the fuse. The bomb had to travel at least 1,000 feet in order to arm the fuse. An arming wire attached to the plane prevented the propeller at the front of the fuse from turning until it was withdrawn when the bomb was released. All of us prior to starting the engine customarily pulled the arming wire and turned the propeller by hand so that the bomb would explode after traveling 500 to 800 feet instead of the entire 1,000 feet. If a bomb had been carried on several missions and not dropped, it was entirely possible for it to be set to explode after 200 to 300 feet. No one wanted to carry a bomb and have it not go off because it had been dropped from too low an altitude to explode.

When you were at 1,000 to 1,500 feet in your dive, you pulled the bomb release and immediately began a sharp pull-out, at the same time closing the dive brakes. Each of the planes had a "G meter," an instrument that shows the number of G's (the force of gravity) you have pulled. On any run on any ship, everyone pulled between nine and twelve G's and went into some stage of a blackout. This was long prior to the G-suit which was designed to help prevent them. Blackouts come in stages. First you have a hard time seeing; then you cannot see at all. At this stage you usually released some pressure on the stick and your sight returned shortly. It is important to remember that it is not only the amount of G's that cause a blackout, but the length of time these forces are present, together with each individual's physical condition. Normally, when your sight returned, the nose of the aircraft was above the horizon and you then pushed the stick forward so as to go right down on the water. You had closed your dive brakes immediately upon releasing the bomb and had picked up a great deal of speed. Your throttle stayed wide open until out of the range of the antiaircraft fire.

The personality of aviation combat has very naturally changed over the years. As a boy I was given a book, "Diary of An Unknown Aviator," by Elliot White Springs. It purports to be and may be the diary of an aviator during the First World War, and it probably is a true story because one of the people written about was Fiorello LaGuardia, who was later the mayor of New York. The book gives details of the dogfights with the primitive aircraft of that day. I was also privileged to spend an afternoon and evening with Eddie Rickenbacker when he came to speak to the local American Legion. Gesturing with his hands to illustrate—in typical pilot fashion—he described the dogfights that led to his becoming the top American ace of World War I. When I was later a squadron commander in the Marshall Islands, my group commander was Col. Chauncey V. Burnett, who had been one of the Marine aviators of that war. In each case, they could describe in detail their combat experience—how parachutes were originally looked upon with disdain, how machine guns were first installed, how the tactics of that day, such as the loop and the Immelmann, evolved. It appeared to be a gentleman's war, and a personal one.

To the Mach 2 fighter pilot of today, I am sure our planes and tactics appear as outmoded as these did to us, and probably more so. It was only about twenty years between the first and second world wars and has been forty since the last one. In our times the enemy fighters were generally found circling high above their ships or bases and were sighted by us as specs in the sky before we reached our targets. We learned to keep our heads up, looking for them, but could only keep flying to the target and wait for them to make the move. There was no way for us to get away from anyone. If we had an escort, our fighters weaved back and forth above us to keep up their speed so that they could either intercept the Japanese before they made their first pass or follow them after they completed their first run. After the initial contact, the fighters were all over the sky, and we were generally forgotten by ours unless they happened to be following a Japanese who was making a second run on us. Generally, in the early days, we had fewer fighters than there were dive-bombers and more Japanese fighters than friendly ones. Later, this was not the case.

After the Japanese pilot had made his first firing pass on us there would be fighting around us, but if the enemy pilot had not been engaged by one of ours he continued to try and harass us. With the twelve guns of the rear-seat gunners of six SBDs they did not generally come in from the rear but tried to wait for us to finish our runs and catch us alone before the rendezvous, when we were the most vulnerable. A quick rendezvous was imperative. The searches where there were only two of us, and in particular a search near a Japanese base, were not healthy.

While our war was not nearly so personal as the first one, it was more personal than the jet aircraft war of Korea and surely of the Vietnam conflict. We could see the pilot who was shooting at us and could see the men on the ships we were attempting to bomb. Our maximum speed was about 160 knots. We could not run away from anybody. Early, we complained about the armor plating that surrounded the pilot because it slowed the plane, but when we came back with 20-mm fragments or 7.7-mm projectiles in this same armor plate, we stopped complaining.

And it was certainly not the gentleman's war I had read about in the first war. As an example, Sam Logan, a classmate in flight school, was flying a fighter while covering us on one of the missions and was shot down. He bailed out and while he was floating down in his parachute the pilot who had shot him down came back to try to hit him with his prop. As Sam told me, on the first two passes he pulled up his feet so that the prop would miss him, but on the third one he thought that the prop would miss and failed to pull up his feet. It hit one of his feet, and he lost a part of that foot. We all carried a syringe of morphine in the web belt that held our pistol, knife, matches, and other emergency supplies in case we were shot down. Sam gave himself a shot, put a tourniquet on his foot, and was able to get into his lifeboat when he hit the water. He was rescued and later was able to continue as a flight instructor, but he was denied his request for another tour of duty overseas.

On one of our trips to Sydney later on, somehow one of the liaison officers with the Royal Australian Air Force found out that we were in town and asked several of us to come out to their field and speak to a squadron of Australian dive-bombing pilots. Dive-bombing had never been used by the Allies in Europe. We were told that these pilots thought that they were being trained as suicide pilots, that their morale was low, and that we should emphasize tactics and survival. They were a fine group of men, and in a short time we became very attached to them. I was chosen to make the talk on tactics and described how the six to twelve of us went out with eight to ten fighters covering us. When I used these figures they laughed. I told them that it was no laughing matter and that they would be glad to have fighters covering them. Their commanding officer, who had fought in the Battle of Britain, interrupted and said that they were not laughing because there were fighters but because he had told them that in Europe on daylight raids three to six heavy bombers were accompanied by 100 fighters. We truly enjoyed our evening with these pilots and all of us agreed that they were the "wildest Indians we had ever seen."

During our first and second tours of duty at Guadalcanal the squadron operations office was a dugout with sandbags and coconut logs and then covered with dirt. Attached to the front was a large tent fly with a table and a blackboard on which were the numbers of the planes and their assignments, whether search, antisub, standby for attack, or out of commission for whatever reason. When you were as-

Squadron operations, with the blackboard for the planes at Guadalcanal, 1942. M. Sgt. George Cicala, the leading chief of the squadron, is seated at left of the board. The operations office is behind the sandbags at right.

signed a mission your name was put on the board together with the plane number assigned. About fifty feet away was the ready tent for the pilots who were not assigned to any particular mission. When an attack mission came down from the group, the operations officer assigned the pilots and the planes and gave the flight leader whatever information had been given to him. The flight leader then briefed the pilots on the mission, giving all of the information he had and a detailed description of the manner in which he intended to approach the target, go into the dive, and rendezvous. Everyone had a chartboard where he put all of the information that he might need: the number of the plane assigned to each of the pilots, the rendezvous information on leaving the field, the course and distance to the target, and any other necessary facts.

Once the briefing was over the pilots and gunners were

taken to the planes by whatever transportation was available, be it jeep, bomb truck, mule (a tractor-like vehicle used to move planes), or whatever. Sometimes this was the most dangerous part of the mission. Everyone was in a hurry and pilots and gunners hung onto the vehicles as best they could with the drivers all trying to emulate Barney Oldfield in getting to the planes in a hurry. When you reached your plane, you made a quick check of the plane, its ordnance, and the parachute, and started it as soon as possible. All of the planes taxied to the end of the runway trying if possible to arrive there in the order of takeoff. Many times it was necessary to change planes for one reason or the other, and it was not always possible to take off in the assigned order.

After takeoff, the flight leader flew straight ahead for about twenty seconds for each plane on the mission and then made a left-hand turn of 180 degrees and headed back to the field until the rendezvous was completed. Each of the planes following turned inside of the leader so that the rendezvous was completed prior to reaching the field.

After the briefing and until the takeoff, tension mounted for each of us, but we all found that after we pushed the throttle for takeoff all of the tension left. Each was concentrating on the mission. The flight leader had to be sure that he led so as not to put any of the other planes in a dangerous or uncomfortable position, had to be sure that he cleared any clouds with enough leeway so that none of the flight was led into them, and that the throttle setting was such that the last plane could maintain its position in the formation. As soon as we had cleared the harbor, we and our gunners each fired a few rounds with our guns to make sure that they were working. The firing mechanism for the front 50-caliber machine guns was in the cockpit with the pilot and some smoke and oil would get in the cockpit when they were fired. After the target was in sight a certain amount of tension returned, and when the antiaircraft fire commenced we were all on our toes.

After the dive-bombing run when you were away from

the antiaircraft guns and any Zeros, if there was no damage to the plane, you felt the biggest high imaginable. With the exception of Horatio Ball and A. B. Marvel, all of us wanted to be on attack missions rather than on any other type. It was a thrill that is hard to explain. None of us felt that we were going to be shot down. It was always going to be someone else.

★ 4 ★

Organization and Deployment of VMSB-132

Marine Corps Aviation certainly began on a shoestring. Two squadrons were sent overseas in World War I. With the coming of the depression of 1930 the entire Marine Corps, ground and aviation, was reduced to about 15,300 officers and men, smaller than the New York City police force. In 1932 the Corps was authorized a total of 130 aviators, but in the following year the number was reduced to 124. By June 30, 1940, aviation had been increased to an authorized allowance of 245 pilots. In January 1941 there were 425 pilots and on June 30, 1941, 453. On December 7, 1941, when Pearl Harbor was attacked 610 pilots were on active duty. A great part of the increase was accomplished by the mobilization in 1940–41 of all of the Marine Reserve pilots in the reserve squadrons. At that time the Marine Corps was assigned 220 aircraft divided into two wings with one Marine Air Group (MAG) each, MAG-11 on the east coast and MAG-21 stationed on various islands in the Pacific. MAG-11 consisted of two fighter squadrons (VMF) and two dive-bombing squadrons (VMSB). The squadrons from MAG-11 were all based at MCAS Quantico. On December 7 three of these squadrons were on maneuvers at New Bern, North Carolina (later to be MCAS Cherry Point), but by December 9 all were on the way to the west coast. Bill Cohron was our squadron intelligence officer later but at that time was a radio gunner. He was on leave and was directed to return to Quantico from which he flew across the country with Joe Sailer, our first commanding officer, and three other planes that were late in leaving because of mechanical difficulty. VMSB-132, one of the original squadrons of MAG-11, was commanded by Maj. Albert D. Cooley at the outbreak of the war. Major Cooley was our group commander (MAG-14) when we reached Guadalcanal and by then was Lieutenant Colonel Cooley. On March 1, 1942, MAG-11 was divided like an amoeba to form MAGs-12, 13, 14, and 15. It is of interest to note that by the end of the war there were 10,049 pilots and 128 squadrons in Marine Aviation.

In September 1942, VMSB-132 was beginning to be fleshed out to an operational squadron again. Joe Sailer had been with the squadron for the entire time since Quantico and was the only accomplished pilot. He had finished flight school in the early thirties and after serving a tour of duty with the regular Marine Corps had transferred to the Floyd Bennett Field reserve squadron at New York City. He was employed by Sperry Gyroscope, where he was one of those who perfected the Norden bombsight that was used for high-level bombing. Prior to his mobilization he had been sent to England by Sperry to help the British with the use of the bombsight. When the reserves were recalled, he returned to active duty.

On about October 10, MAG-11, including VMSB-132 and 142, and VMF-112 and 122 was alerted to board the *Lurline* for overseas assignment. Every man was to mark his gear with the designation given to each squadron—our insignia being a black half-circle with the letter B in the middle. We all very carefully stenciled this on footlockers, seabags, and our hand luggage. I was given the duty of picking up these items and delivering them to the *Lurline* at the dock in San Diego. I had purchased a 1931 Plymouth coupe for seventy-five dollars after arriving in San Diego. When I was leaving the BOQ to collect the gear of the others, the laundry man happened to be there. I sold my car to him for five dollars, bought a quart of whiskey, and put it in my footlocker. Walt Eck and Bill Hronek had purchased a Cord automobile which was in great condition. When they could not get any used-car dealer to give them what they thought it was worth, they drove it to the docks, threw the keys into San Diego Bay, and boarded the ship, leaving the Cord parked at the docks. We departed in the morning of October 13. Although we carried our winter flight gear, we all suspected that we were going to the Solomons.

The *Lurline* was the queen of the Matson Line. Except for the conversion of the ship for troop convoy, it was still a beautiful ship. There were eight bunks in the small staterooms where the junior officers were quartered. Our enlisted men were bunked on the decks four high. There were 6,000 troops on her, some as replacements for Guadalcanal. The officers took their meals in the passengers' dining room and were served by the stewards of the peacetime cruises. Since we ordered from the menu of those cruises, the food was out of this world. Our steward, John, saw to us as though we were his peacetime passengers and would serve us anything we wanted.

The trip over was uneventful. The speed of the ship was so great that we were not in convoy. If we saw any smoke or anything of interest on the horizon we merely turned tail and left it behind. As soon as we were out of sight of land most of the troops became seasick, and for a few days I believe we could have been located by the smell that permeated the entire ship. One of my roommates was Andy Jackson, who had a classic case—so bad that he turned green. We were assigned watches on the decks below where the replacement troops for Guadalcanal were billeted. Jackson was assigned the two-to-four watch on D deck below the water line and because of his condition, I took the watch for him. Some time during the watch, Maj. Louis B. Robertshaw, our executive officer, came by to inspect the watch. In answer to his questions as to why I was there rather than Jackson, I told him about Jackson's problem, and his reply was to the effect that Marine officers did not get seasick and for me to go and get Jackson. I finally, despite the protestations of Andy, was able to get him up. I can still see him doing the side-straddle hop at exercise the next day.

On October 28 we arrived at Noumea, New Caledonia. None of us had ever heard of New Caledonia. Investigation after the war revealed a fascinating island. It was discovered by Captain Cook on one of his famous voyages. It is an island 240 miles long and an average of about 30 miles wide with mountains rising to 6,000 feet running the entire length. It lies about 1,200 nautical miles northeast of Sydney, Australia. As was the case with most of the islands, the natives practiced cannibalism until after the beginning of the twentieth century. It was governed by the French and was used as a penal colony from the Franco-Prussian War until the beginning of World War II. Following the surrender of France in World War II, it was ruled by a government sympathetic to Vichy. When the allies came on the island in the spring of 1942, the loyalty of the local people and the government was regarded as questionable, and strict censorship of all communications was imposed.

There were several damaged ships in the harbor, and for the first time we realized that we had arrived at THE WAR. One of the warships, a cruiser, had suffered heavy damage in a naval battle at Guadalcanal. Her superstructure and guns showed evidence of having been hit several times by large guns. All of the personnel on the starboard side of our ship were called to attention and ordered to salute the damaged ship while the *Lurline*'s whistle was blown three times. The intercom announced the name of the damaged ship and told us that she had participated gallantly in one of the naval battles. One of the merchant ships in the harbor had been hit, causing a hole to be blown through both sides below the waterline, and while we were watching the ships, a boat with an outboard motor went through it.

We stayed on the *Lurline* for two or three days and then disembarked to tents set up on a hill overlooking the city. It was a quaint little island town but none of us except Archie D. "Hap" Simpson had the curiosity to go and see the sights. I know that it had a leper colony; we saw some Catholic priests walking around the town and I remember a small, picturesque church. Although we came back to the island on each of our rest leaves en route to Sydney, we were then at Tontouta Airfield which was about fifty or seventy-five miles to the northeast, and we never had another opportunity to explore the town.

Major Sailer, Tex Kelly, Wayne Gentry, and Pete Nawman left for Guadalcanal on the day we disembarked. They arrived at the Canal on November 1 and Wayne and Pete were killed on their second hop on November 2. Walt Eck and Bill Hronek went to Guadalcanal November 3. The remainder of us continued to live in the tents outside Noumea for about two days.

Before Major Sailer and the others left, we cut cards to determine in what order we would go to Guadalcanal. I remember that I cut the eight of hearts and was the next to go after Eck and Hronek. After Major Sailer had gone, Major Robertshaw called all of the pilots to the mess tent and gave us navigation problems to redetermine the order of going. The first one to finish a problem would be the next to go. I was the first to finish the first problem and remained the next to get to go. The next day, Horatio Ball, George Herlihy, Russ Janson, Charlie Kollman, Hap Simpson, Jack Sperzel, Sgt. Ed Wallof, and I left with Major Robertshaw.

The ride from Noumea to the airfield at Tontouta was memorable. We were in the back of a truck with no springs, on a road that was nothing more than a trail. We arrived at the airfield and were promptly flown about 400 miles to the island of Espiritu Santo in the New Hebrides (code name "Buttons"). Some of the SBDs from the carrier *Hornet,* which had been sunk in the Battle of the Santa Cruz Islands about ten days earlier, were there, and we were to fly them to Guadalcanal. They were among the last ones left and were in terrible condition. The plane that Hap Simpson flew was wrinkled from just aft of the wing to the tail. All of the others were in equally bad condition.

We were each allowed to fly a test hop in the plane we were to take, and not one of us turned a plane down. If we had, we might not have been able to get another, and we were all eager to get there. There were no aviation charts of the area, and there was only one sea navigational chart for all of us. Very naturally this was given to Major Robertshaw, the flight leader. It showed all of the hazards to sea navigation and the depth of the ocean. If for any reason anyone had had to ditch, we would have known at least the depth of the ocean.

There were no radio aids to navigation of any kind at any of the airfields. No radios controlled traffic around the field. The tower at Espiritu was located in a large tree by the runway. Its only control was a red or green light or a "Very pistol" which could shoot a charge very much like a Roman candle, red or green as the occasion might demand. After spending two nights here, the eight of us were briefed for the flight to Guadalcanal. We were to fly formation on an R4D, a Douglas transport (also known as a DC3), for the navigation to Henderson Field at "Cactus" (the code name for Guadalcanal). Our seabags, which we had brought with us, were put on the R4D. We were meticulously briefed to be especially careful to maintain a tight traffic circle around the field when we arrived. If we strayed and made a wide traffic circle we would be over the Japanese lines and would be subject to small arms fire and light antiaircraft. It made an impression on all of us.

We took off about noon and flew formation on the R4D. If we ran into bad weather we were to fly a tight formation on the transport so we would not get lost. The weather within ten degrees of the equator is changeable and unpredictable. There are no weather fronts within this area, but there are periods of violent thunderstorms which cover miles, and flying under such conditions was not to be desired. Fortunately, the weather gave us no problem on the flight up, and after about four and one-half hours we sighted the southeastern tip of Guadalcanal.

★ 5 ★

October at Guadalcanal

A number of significant events preceded our arrival at the Canal. The portion of the First Marine Division stationed at Camp LeJeune, North Carolina, was transported through the Panama Canal in May of 1942 and landed in Wellington, New Zealand, on June 14. Between June 4 and June 7 we fought the Battle of Midway, in which the Japanese lost four of their big carriers to one of ours. After a short time ashore in New Zealand, the division re-embarked. A decision had been made by the Joint Chiefs that the Marines were to recapture Tulagi, the Santa Cruz Islands, and adjacent positions. Guadalcanal was not mentioned in the order. No one knew anything about that part of the world in a military sense. Gen. A. A. Vandegrift sent his intelligence officer to Australia in an attempt to get what information he could from some of the planters who had left the area when it was obvious that it was to be taken by the enemy. An Army Air Force B-17 from New Caledonia carrying the division air officer made an attempt to take some pictures of the area, but the plane was driven off by some float Zeros based at Tulagi. Other parts of the division were still at sea being transported from the west coast. One of its regiments was on garrison duty at Samoa. Three carriers, the *Saratoga, Enterprise,* and *Wasp,* were to cover the landings. It was recognized that five or six days would be needed to unload the cargo ships, but the carriers were only committed for two days and actually stayed for only thirty-six hours.

The field at Guadalcanal was not completed. The Japanese had begun at each end, and the middle was not yet finished. The Marines landed at Guadalcanal on August 7 and took the airfield on August 8 without any trouble. Most of the Japanese troops there were construction battalions with only a limited number of naval landing troops, the Japanese marines. All of them evacuated the airfield leaving their equipment and supplies. It was this equipment which the U.S. Marine engineers used to finish the field. The cargo ships left after three days and took with them most of the heavy equipment and many of the supplies needed by the Marines.

On the night of August 8 there was a naval battle in the harbor. We lost four cruisers, the *Chicago, Vincennes, Quincy,* and an Australian cruiser, the *Canberra.* The Japanese did not lose a ship but made a mistake in not continuing and sinking all of the transports and cargo ships. They did not know that the carriers had already left, nor did they recognize the limited strength of the Marines. During the month of August they sent small detachments of 1,000 to 1,500 men to attempt to retake the island. Most of these were landed in the Koli Point area east of the airfield, but there was no significant fighting until the afternoon of August 21 at the Tenaru River, where the Marines wiped out the first attempt to retake the airfield.

The airfield was completed and on August 20 the first planes, VMSB-232 under Lt. Col. Richard Mangrum and one of the fighter squadrons of MAG-23, landed on the field. Prior to that time the Japanese had had complete control of the air and the sea in the entire area. They had, with impunity, landed reinforcements and shelled the beach. After August 20 and until the middle of November they controlled the sea at night, but during the day the air over the field was controlled by the Marines.

The nearest enemy airfield was at Rabaul, New Guinea, and the Japanese aircraft, in order to reach Guadalcanal, had to fly almost 600 miles and return. At this distance their fighters had to carry belly tanks which could not be released, and few of the crippled planes could return to base. This loss of their better pilots was felt as the war progressed. By contrast, because we were fighting over our own territory and were assisted by the coastwatcher network, many of our pilots who were shot down were able to return to fight another day.

Following the battle at the Tenaru, the first serious attempt by the Japanese to retake the airfield resulted in the Battle of Bloody Ridge. During the last week in August and the first part of September, they had placed about 4,500 crack troops ashore in the Koli Point area and they advanced inland rather than along the beach as in the Tenaru battle. On September 13 and 14 a battle was fought at Bloody Ridge in which the Japanese were almost successful. Some of them actually reached the division command post, but the final outcome was another victory for the Marines with terrific losses to the enemy. (Of the battle of Bloody Ridge, Morison, in his *History of United States Naval Operations in World War II,* says: "The Battle of the Ridge was one of the crucial ground actions of the Pacific War. It was won by Edson's inspired leadership, and the skill and courage of individual Marines. If this battle had been lost, Henderson Field would have been lost, and the Marines would have been hard put to hold the island.")

In the interim, the losses in pilots and aircraft were substantial. VMSB-231, commanded by Maj. Leo R. Smith, the remaining dive-bomber squadron in MAG-23, and its remaining fighter squadron, VMF-224, were sent to the island. These squadrons carried the load until the end of September when pilots from VMSB-141 out of MAG-14 began to arrive. It is of interest to note that when VMSB-232 was finally evacuated on October 12, of the twelve pilots who had arrived with the squadron, only Lieutenant Colonel Mangrum was able to fly. VMSB-231, the second dive-bombing squadron, had commenced operations on August 31 with seventeen pilots and was relieved on October 16 with only five pilots in a flight status.

The third dive-bombing squadron committed to Guadalcanal was VMSB-141. It left the States on September 1 and arrived at Noumea on September 22. It immediately began to feed its pilots into the two SBD squadrons on the

Canal. It was a big squadron consisting of forty-one pilots, with training typical of most of the squadrons. Lt. John Shepard had fewer than ten hours in the SBD when he reached Guadalcanal, including the time he accumulated when he was catapulted off the carrier for the flight to Cactus. Of its forty-one pilots, eventually eleven were missing in action, seven were killed in action, and nine were evacuated for illness or injuries. Fourteen pilots were finally evacuated on November 14. The squadron lost five commanding officers from October 13 through November 14. According to a report submitted by its flight surgeon, Dr. Victor S. Falk, Jr., "A number of pertinent factors arise in considering the heavy losses among these pilots. Many of them had joined the squadron just before it left the States and they had less than 10 hours in dive bombers. While they were at Guadalcanal, the frequent enemy night bombing raids interfered with their much-needed rest. The food situation was generally poor. It was necessary to eat whenever the galley was in operation. Since the firing of ranges before dawn was not permitted, it was impossible to have hot chow preceding early morning hops. Facilities for meals at the ready tent were inadequate because of the lack of ranges and the difficulty of transporting prepared food from distant galleys. Operations from Henderson Field was further complicated by the heavy field artillery, known as Pistol Pete. These guns had the runway boresighted. The loss of senior officers and the consequent lack of leadership made the pilots feel as if there were no one looking out for them."

When our pilots returned to the States, we brought back the enlisted from this squadron, and I was proud to have the privilege of serving as its CO and reorganizing the squadron at MCAS El Toro in the fall of 1943.

The Navy was fast losing its aircraft carriers during this same period. The *Enterprise* was hit by a dive-bomber during the Battle of the Eastern Solomons on August 24 and her forward elevator was unreliable for the rest of the year. The *Saratoga* was torpedoed by a submarine on August 27 and out of action for about three months. On September 15, the *Wasp* was torpedoed and sunk. The *Hornet* was sunk by enemy dive-bombers in the Battle of the Santa Cruz Islands on October 26. By November 1 the only operational carrier was the *Enterprise*, and the recalcitrant forward elevator greatly restricted her operational ability.

Following the September debacle, the Japanese staff held a number of joint Army-Navy meetings to determine the next steps to be taken. Their Navy, owing to its losses to dive-bombers, was reluctant to commit important surface units to the retaking of the island and wanted instead to transport the troops and equipment by barges in what came to be known as the "rat patrol." The Japanese Army was insistent that troops be sent as a unit since it had now determined to send a complete division with its attendant artillery, including 150-mm guns. Admiral Yamamoto finally interceded and agreed to escort the troopships with his battleships and all necessary naval support. Special shells with thin exteriors and instantaneous fuses were manufactured in Japan to be used in the bombardment of the airfield. These shells detonated when striking the palm trees, sending fragments to destroy men and planes. At this time there were approximately 5,000 Japanese troops scattered about the island and about 17,000 Marines there and at Tulagi.

During the first week in October the enemy landed their entire Second Division and the staff of the Seventeenth Army. When General Hyakutake saw the condition of the Japanese troops left on the island, he sent a message to Rabaul regarding the conditions and asked for more troops and supplies at once. A recent battle at the Matanikau River, west of the field, also made a new battle plan necessary. The planned attack would not be executed only along the coast line but would be coordinated with a major attack from inland in the area where the Battle of Bloody Ridge had been fought, on this occasion with far greater numbers of men and better equipment. Meanwhile, Rabaul, in answer to the plea of General Hyakutake, sent two seaplane tenders and a number of destroyers with the heavy artillery and additional men. This task force was accompanied by three cruisers and was sighted on the afternoon of October 11 by a B-17. For the first time since the unfortunate battle of Savo Island, the Navy determined to meet the enemy, and the night action resulted in a victory for us, our first. A Japanese cruiser and a destroyer were sunk while we lost only one destroyer, the *Duncan*.

During the naval battle, however, the enemy seaplane tenders and destroyers landed all of the men and supplies without hindrance. By the next morning, October 12, the big guns were ashore and in place along the Matanikau River and were now able to reach the airfield. These guns, 150 mm, were bigger and thereby had greater range than any of the Marines', and consequently could not be brought under fire by them. They were a constant source of concern, and in later days several patrols were sent out for the purpose of disabling them but without success. A bombardment of the airfield scheduled for that night was postponed for one night.

On October 13, a regiment of the Americal Division landed. These were the first Army troops to participate in the operation. There was apparently a cause for optimism. There were about forty SBDs and an equal number of F4Fs, together with several Navy TBFs and sufficient gasoline for normal flight operations. VMSB-141 had arrived with its forty-one pilots. It is worthy of note that the sinking of our carriers and the damage to others was a Godsend to the Marines because most of the dive-bomber replacement planes were from the lost carriers. The optimism was short-lived. At about noon a flight of twenty-four Japanese twin-engine bombers (Bettys) made an unexpected and accurate attack on the airfield from 30,000 feet. There had been no warning by either the coastwatchers or radar. Two hours later, when the planes that had tried to reach the first bombers were being refueled, a second attack by fifteen more Bettys came, leaving the field in shambles. At about the time the Seabees were repairing the damage to the field from the second raid, Pistol Pete opened up for the first time. The heavy artillery which had landed on the eleventh was now in position.

While all of this was going on, two enemy battleships and their escorting cruisers and destroyers were en route to Guadalcanal with the new high explosive and incendiary shells. They arrived offshore at about midnight of October 13–14 and launched their spotting planes. At about one o'clock the first salvo was fired from the fourteen-inch guns of the battleships *Kongo* and *Haruna*. The spotting planes marked the area of fire by a red flare at one end of the runway and a green one at the other. The two ships fired for one hour and thirty-seven minutes, firing 918 rounds, 625 of armor piercing and 293 of the new high explosive.

Admiral Tanaka, one of the Japanese admirals, wrote of this attack: "The ensuing scene baffled description as the fires and explosions from the 36-cm shell hits on the airfield set off enemy planes, fuel dumps, and ammunition storage places. The scene was topped off by flare bombs from our observation planes flying over the field, the whole spectacle making the Ryogoku fireworks display seem like mere child's play. The night's pitch dark was transformed by fire into the brightness of day. Spontaneous cries and shouts of excitement ran throughout the ships." On the airfield, the effect had been devastating. While it seems incredible, only about forty persons were killed. Most of these were aviation personnel including the commanding officer, executive officer, operations officer, and two other pilots of VMSB-141. All of the surviving pilots of the squadron were second lieutenants. Of the SBDs, only seven were not destroyed. All of the Navy TBFs were demolished. Most of the gasoline was lost, and the airfield was completely devastated and unfit for flight operations. The only field that could be used was the dirt fighter strip which had suffered comparably little damage. This field had been completed during October. There were still thirty F4Fs operational but only 4 SBDs.

On October 14 six more transports with the remainder

of General Hyakutake's troops left the Shortland Islands for Guadalcanal. Only a feeble attempt was made to stop them. The four SBDs took off from the fighter strip but they caused no damage. During the night of October 14–15 the cruisers of the enemy's Eighth Fleet unleashed a similar bombardment with their eight-inch guns for more than an hour while the unloading commenced. At dawn, in full view of the Marines, the transports continued their unloading, with destroyers and small boats assisting. Their landing was covered by Zeros circling overhead much as they would have done at one of the islands controlled by the Japanese. There was such a shortage of gasoline that the damaged planes were drained, including a B-17 which was damaged when it landed for repairs. Miraculously, 400 drums of gasoline were discovered in a disposal area which had been forgotten in all of the confusion. Only three of the SBDs were now able to fly. In attempting a takeoff on the fighter strip, Lt. Robert M. Patterson of 141 ran one of these into a shell hole, but he was given a second plane. On becoming airborne in the second, he found that he was not able to retract his wheels and the dive brakes would not operate. Despite these difficulties he was able to make a glide-bombing attack and hit one of the unloading transports. Maj. Jack Cram took General Geiger's PBY (a big twin-engine amphibious flying boat) and after some instruction from one of the fighter pilots whose brother was a torpedo pilot in the Navy, made a torpedo run on the unloading transports. By noon the maintenance personnel were able to get about twelve SBDs ready to fly, and the first sustained attack was launched. In this and subsequent attacks three of the transports were set afire and had to be run aground. The remaining three left at about three o'clock. All of the troops and most of the supplies had been unloaded.

After these setbacks, a general gloom settled over the island. Adm. Chester Nimitz said in his top secret estimate: "It now appears that we are unable to control the sea in the Guadalcanal area. Thus our supply of the positions will only be done at great expense to us. The situation is not hopeless, but it is certainly critical." Secretary of the Navy Frank Knox, when asked to comment on the situation, said that he "would not make any predictions, but every man will give a good account of himself." And later, "Everybody hopes that we can hold on." The estimates of the Japanese strength were now 26,000 troops, and later investigation proved this to be accurate. Adm. Aubrey W. Fitch, the commander of land-based aviation in the South Pacific, passed on to Adm. Robert L. Ghormley, the naval commander, South Pacific area, an estimate from Vandegrift's staff, "that the Jap has moved in and emplaced artillery of longer range than his which is shelling his positions and the airfield at will; that enemy surface craft move at will in the surrounding waters and shell his position destructively both day and night; and that he will be unable indefinitely to hold these positions if this continues."

As one of the answers to these critical questions, on October 18 Admiral Nimitz relieved Admiral Ghormley and appointed Adm. William F. Halsey as COMSOPAC (Commander South Pacific). Reaction among the aviators was enthusiastic. It was said that they now had one of their own in charge. The prior commanders were not naval aviators as was Admiral Halsey. One of the common sayings among the pilots was that Halsey would turn a task force around to find a lost pilot. Justified or not, he certainly had the reputation for carrying the attack to the enemy. On October 24, President Roosevelt sent a message to each of the Joint Chiefs of Staff in which he insisted that reinforcements be provided quickly.

The enemy planned the coordinated attack from the north along the beach and from the west over the old Bloody Ridge area, for October 22. In order to get the troops in position to attack from this latter area, it was necessary for a trail of about four or five miles to be cut through the jungle, across Mount Austin, from the Tassafaranga-Cape Esperance area. Gen. Hyakutake seriously underestimated the difficulty of this undertaking, and the attack was postponed until the twenty-fourth. Because of a breakdown in communications, the beach attack across the Matanikau from the north commenced on the twenty-third. The result was a defeat for the enemy. When the second and primary attack was begun on October 24, the Marines were able to rush reinforcements to the extended lines in the Bloody Ridge area from the troops in the beach area. Hyakutake was so confident of surrender that an operation order was prematurely drawn with all of the details of how and where General Vandegrift would surrender and how the surrender would be accepted. A signal of one green rocket followed by a white and another green was to be given when the airfield was taken. The code word to be sent to Rabaul was "Banzai, objective taken." In error the code words were sent, and the next morning, October 25, in broad daylight, two Japanese destroyers were sent into the harbor to furnish support for the troops. Three cruisers and several other destroyers were also dispatched but the error was discovered and quickly corrected. In the interim, two of the harbor craft were sunk by the enemy destroyers. The cruisers were recalled and the destroyers left without incident because of all the confusion at the field. The attack on the field from the Bloody Ridge area continued for two days but was finally repulsed on the twenty-sixth. Two enemy generals and many troops were killed. The second determined attack on the field had been repulsed.

★ 6 ★

The Island

Guadalcanal from the air is a beautiful island. It is about eighty miles long and twenty miles wide with mountains rising to 8,000 feet in the center. There were no such beaches as on many South Pacific islands. The sands were black and not very wide. At places on the plains next to the ocean, palm trees were planted in rows; otherwise the jungle foliage grew almost to the sea. When we first looked at the island it appeared very peaceful. Henderson Field was about sixty miles from its southeastern tip.

On sighting land, the eight of us moved into a defensive formation and continued up the coast to the field and upon reaching the field, made our approach to land, mindful of the warning given to us at Espiritu regarding straying into a wide traffic pattern. Major Robertshaw, as the flight leader, was first to land. Each of us followed, allowing sufficient time for the plane in front to clear the runway. The major ran off the runway at the end of his landing rollout and consequently our landing pattern was interrupted. Not knowing the front line positions, we all milled around the harbor between Guadalcanal and the Florida Islands until we could each individually make a tight approach to the field and land.

The field at that time had a steel interlocking surface of pierced steel planking called "Marston matting" which did anything but add to its beauty. But the matting gave a surface that was good for landing, especially after a rain. The remainder of the field was anything but imposing. There were no real taxiways. Planes were scattered over about forty acres out in a field. It was the rainy season, and mud and dirt were everywhere. It was said of the area that

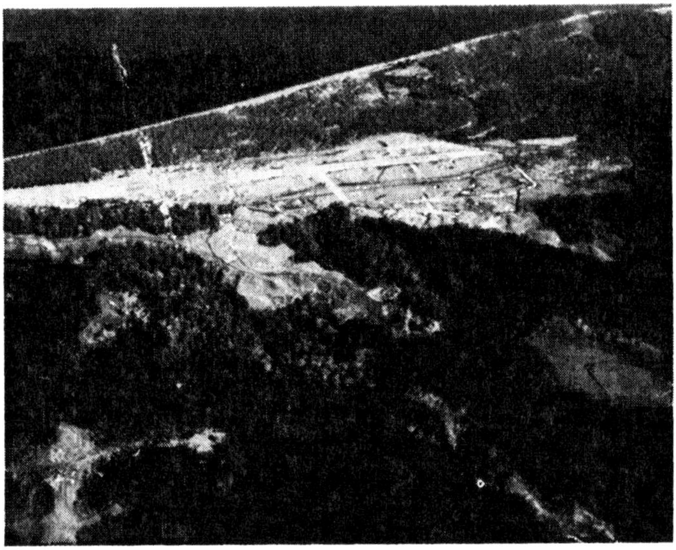

Henderson Field in November 1942.

it was the only place on earth where you could stand in mud to your ankles and get dust in your face. Jack London, the author, had visited the area earlier and said that it was a good description of Hell.

Our planes were serviced by a Navy Carrier Air Service Unit and by VMSB-141 personnel. After I landed, a flatbed truck with 55-gallon drums of gasoline on its back drove up to my plane. The driver got out of the truck and climbed on the wing to help me out of the plane, and he was a friend from Bessemer that I had known all my life. He was with the Navy Unit. Gas was put into the plane with a hand pump from the drums and filtered through a chamois skin. After that initial meeting I never saw Jack Hood until after the war and we both had come home.

The engineering officer of VMSB-141 was Lt. William L. Woodruff, "Bobby" to us. He did a remarkable job under the circumstances. As you would expect, there was no hangar and nowhere to work on the planes except in the field where they were parked. Bobby was an old-time Marine, commissioned from the ranks, and was used to getting things done. His enlisted men were crazy about him and would work from daylight to dark to get as many planes as possible ready for the next flights. When the Japanese left, after the landings, they left all of their equipment, and Bobby and his men improvised in every way for the things necessary for the engine changes and the like. Bobby told me that one of the planes was numbered "13" and that pilots either turned it down or brought it back from missions with something wrong until he changed the number to "18" by painting the "3" to an "8." After that he said it was not brought back any more than any other.

When the Japanese left the field they abandoned a 1940 four-door Plymouth automobile. I am sure that it was the staff car for the Japanese commander. The fuel pump had gone bad, and Bobby had solved that problem by putting the gas tank on top of the car. It was his car, and he went all around carrying parts and crews to planes at various points on the field. After our first tour of duty, I never saw the car again.

After landing, we all went to the dugout and tent that served as squadron operations. Here for the first time we learned that Wayne Gentry and Pete Nawman had been lost. On their second flight, they had volunteered to search for and attack some Japanese ships which had been reported. With Lt. Com. John Eldrige, the commanding officer of a Navy squadron, VS-71, from one of the carriers, they took off at dusk and in bad weather. All three were lost. Their bodies were found later on Santa Isabel, one of the other islands of the Solomon group. In the dark and bad weather they had flown into the mountains. (In 1944, two destroyer escorts were named in honor of these two, destroyer escort 416, the *Melvin R. Nawman,* and destroyer escort 349, the *Gentry.*) We also were told that Walt Eck had dropped a depth charge and forced a Japanese sub onto the beach at the northern end of the island.

Each of us took our plotting boards and drew a map of

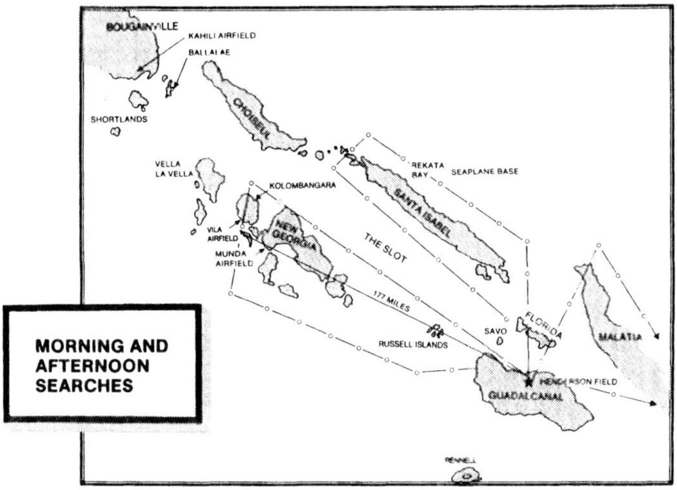

the islands to assist in the navigation. We were then taken to our newly erected tents. The pilots of our squadron who had preceded us had moved into the area where VMSB-141, the squadron we were to relieve, was living. These camps were near each other on Bloody Ridge, the area where the hardest fighting had taken place. Ours was a new area; the paths were cut out of the jungle, and a place for each of the tents was cleared. Except for these paths, it was impossible to walk. It had the advantage of being clean as opposed to the 141 area, which had been used for some time. This was the last time for almost ten days that many of us saw, in daylight, the tents where we lived. The camps were about a mile by road from the flight office and on the opposite side of the field. Directly from the field it was less than a quarter of a mile. Each morning we were awakened at about 3:30 to go to the operations tent where we had breakfast—a breakfast of powdered eggs, which none of us could eat, one slice of bread, jelly, and coffee with no sugar or cream. Until Major Robertshaw complained to the group, the early flights had taken off without any breakfast. Morning searches took off just before daylight. Pilots who were not on a search stood by for an attack or any mission necessary, an antisub patrol, artillery spotting, a message drop, or an engine test. We returned to our tents after dark following the afternoon searches.

On our second night there, one of the line Marines, a part of a patrol, came very cautiously into our tent area with his rifle at the ready and said that some Japanese had slipped through the front lines and might be in our area. The front lines were about a quarter of a mile past our tents and we could hear intermittent machine guns, rifles firing, hand grenades exploding, and the like. The line Marine did not add to our comfort. I was in a tent with Jug Herlihy, Russ Janson, and Chuck Kollman. Each of us had had a 45-caliber automatic issued to us. Normally all of us slept in our flight suits, taking off only our shoes. That night I very carefully put a round in the chamber of my forty-five and put it under my pillow, ready for any eventuality. Some time during the night, I heard a noise in the jungle behind the tent which sounded as though someone were crawling in the underbrush. I knew, of course, that I was the only one who was awake and I very slowly and cautiously took the pistol from under my pillow. The noise continued and seemed to get closer. As quietly as possible I put the pistol in the sleeping bag with me to muffle the sound and cocked the gun. There was a perceptible click, followed by click, click, click as the others in the tent cocked theirs, also. All had been awake and had heard that same noise. The noise stopped. I hate to imagine what would have happened if there had been someone there and he had shaken the tent. We would probably have killed each other.

Everything we had was in our seabags, canvas oversized garbage bags. We were told not to use a light of any kind, and when we lit a cigarette to hide the light with our hands. Once Major Robertshaw, who was in the tent next to ours, could not find something in his seabag in the dark. The line troops were still patrolling the area. The major turned his flashlight on, shining it into his seabag and a rifle shot was fired through the woods near the tents. None of us ever turned on a flashlight again. On November 14 when ships were shelling us, a shell almost hit the tents. It was a dud, but we abandoned this living area and moved into tents that were erected in the 141 area. One of the nice things about the first area was that we did not have to dig foxholes because the line Marines who had been there previously had already dug them for us. In the 141 area it was necessary to dig our own, all foxholes being taken.

For the first four or five days, things were relatively calm. We flew sector searches. On these missions there were usually two planes and the purpose was to look for Japanese shipping, barges, or for anything of interest. Most of us were led on these missions by the 141 pilots the first time, and they were generally very tiring missions of about three-and-a-half to four-hour duration. One of these went around Santa Isabel, another around New Georgia and Kolombangara, and a third around Malatia, other islands in the Solomon group. The Japanese had a seaplane base at Rekata Bay on the northern side of Santa Isabel which added some interest to that search because Zeros on floats were based there on occasion. If one drew the Santa Isabel search, he hoped for some sort of cloud cover so as to get away if the Japanese planes came up. I never found any planes at Rekata on my search but I remember the respect in which it was held by John Shepard, the 141 pilot who led me on my first search, which was Santa Isabel.

We also flew antisub patrols in the harbor. These were the most boring flights of all. The harbor consisted of the area between Guadalcanal and the Florida Islands, and the patrol extended northwest to Savo, a small island in the center of "the slot." This area was about ten by twenty miles. On one of these flights one flew at 500 to 1,000 feet and looked for submarines or survivors of the naval battles. Except for Walt Eck, no one ever saw a sub, and Walt found his on a sector search and not on a sub patrol. But I must admit that, in the middle of the day, in the middle of the harbor, a sub sank a merchant ship unloading supplies. I never thought to ask who was on antisub patrol that day.

Generally near the middle of the day there was a bombing raid of some kind by nine to eighteen twin-engine bombers coming in at about 30,000 feet. The fighters would intercept and usually shot one or more down. Sometimes one of the wings of the bomber fluttered down much like a falling leaf. From back in the hills, Pistol Pete would fire an intermittent round that fell somewhere on the field. It very obviously was a long way away as its accuracy was poor. I never remember it hitting anything, though it was a bit disconcerting. Every night, almost without exception, "Washing Machine Charlie" came over. This was a twin-engined bomber which was given this name because its engines were never synchronized. Though searchlights came on and antiaircraft fired I do not remember that any Charlie was ever shot down. Sometimes the antiaircraft gave a real show, particularly if the plane came in low so that the smaller guns could fire. The shows from Tulagi (across the harbor in the Florida Islands) were the best. In the beginning everyone always went into a foxhole but later we learned to try to find the plane in the searchlights and if it was not coming directly over us, we enjoyed the excitement. On one occasion during night standby at the field, five or six of us were watching the searchlights on the plane and the shooting when, without warning, we heard the whistling sound of a bomb. We knew it was close and tried to make the operations dugout. We would have made it but for a Navy captain who was visiting and had never heard a bomb. He was standing in the entrance to operations. He didn't recognize the sound and didn't know he should move. When we ran into him we all fell in a heap at the entrance to the dugout. The bomb was close, and dirt fell on us. Captain Butts arose, dusted himself off, and said something about the "damn fool Marines." (He later was promoted to admiral. I served with him in Washington.) No one in our squadron was ever killed or injured by

An SBD after it had been hit by a Japanese bomb. The plane had been pushed into the edge of the coconut grove in an attempt to conceal it from the bombers.

the bombings, though one of the bombs fell in the area next to ours and killed a number of people. Occasionally the bombs would hit a plane and the fire of the burning plane would cause its bomb to explode.

On one occasion, two B-24s, large four-engine Army bombers, had landed at the field just before dark. They were fully loaded and had probably four 1,000-pound bombs in each of their bomb bays. They were parked close together. Washing Machine Charlie hit one of them and set it on fire, and it spread to the other. The machine gun ammunition was going off from the heat of the fire with the tracers going in every direction. We were all watching from about 300 to 400 yards when the bombs of the first plane exploded. The shock wave almost knocked us off our feet. When the bombs from the second went off, we all fell to the ground. It was quite a show.

On November 10 while I was on an antisub patrol, a report of the sighting of some enemy destroyers came, and Major Sailer led the first squadron attack on ships. The weather was bad and the results, as reported in the squadron diary, were undetermined. One report is that one of the 141 pilots still flying with us hit one of them. The Japanese reports indicate that the destroyers *Takanami* and *Naganami* were damaged and were forced to turn back. I was terribly disappointed that I did not get to go on that bombing flight.

My diary for November 12 reads, "We hear that there is lots coming down our way. The Japs like the 13th. Had a bombing raid but nothing very exciting." The scuttlebutt was correct. The next three days were days none of us will ever forget.

⋆ 7 ⋆

November 12–15

Winston Churchill is reputed to have said, "Nothing in life is so exhilarating as to be shot at without results." I am sure that all of us who have had the experience will agree. Between November 12 and 15, each of us had enough of these exhilarating experiences to last a lifetime.

At the end of October the situation on Guadalcanal was most desperate. We were the air replacements thrown into the gap, the only replacements available. The ground troops on the *Lurline* with us, the 8th Marines, were sent on to Cactus by ship and arrived about November 4. They were a welcome addition.

Beginning about November 9, the Marines had attacked along the Matanikau River to the west of the airfield in an attempt to move the front lines away from the field so that Pistol Pete could not reach it. After two days they decided that they could not hold the gains they had made, and they were withdrawn from the ground taken. Some of us furnished spotting planes for the artillery during the attack and the withdrawal. On November 11 two waves of Japanese planes had made attacks on ships in the harbor and at Tulagi. In the first of these, at 0930, nine Val dive-bombers from the carrier *Hiyo* escorted by eighteen Zeros attacked four transports which were bringing in an Army regiment, the second such regiment intended for replacement of the Marines who had been there since August. Our fighters shot down four Zeros and five dive-bombers but lost six F4Fs and four pilots. This resulted from the quality of the Japanese carrier pilots, as opposed to the Japanese Army replacement pilots who were now beginning to operate in the area from airfields on Bougainville.

At about 1100, twenty-seven Bettys accompanied by twenty-six Zeros attacked the field. VMF-121 shot down four bombers at a cost of one plane and pilot. It was a hard day for VMF-121, with the loss of five pilots. For the dive-bombers it was a day of some excitement, much interest, and little action other than the usual searches.

On November 12, the first action of any kind was a vigorous depth charge attack on a submarine contact at about 0600 by one of our destroyers. This was followed by Pistol Pete's shelling of more Marine replacements, who were unloading from four transports just arrived in the harbor. The destroyers were able to silence him for the time being, but at about 1330 a report came from a coast-watcher that enemy bombers and fighters were on the way. At 1405 enemy planes were sighted just east of the Florida Islands preparing for a torpedo run on the ships in the harbor. Those of us on the ground were treated to a high-level attack by nine of the Bettys from altitude without hindrance, since protection of the ships had priority for the fighters. To add to the excitement, nine dive-bombers made a coordinated attack on the transports at this same time. None of the ships was hit and the only damage to the field was holes in the landscape. The fighters cleaned up, shooting down all but one of the Bettys on the torpedo attack at a cost of three F4Fs, all of whose pilots were saved.

Our squadron diary for November 12, among the search reports and the reports of the planes downed from the attacks of the Japanese, says: "While on a sector search, Lieutenants Hronek and Eck sighted a Japanese force of two small aircraft carriers (probably converted carriers), and two destroyers, bearing two hundred sixty-five (265) degrees. One aircraft carrier had a number of planes on the flight deck. Exceptionally bad weather and rain squalls made further identification of these and sighting of other probable units impossible. One plane's radio transmitter failed to function and the other plane could not raise the Henderson Field radio station; thus both planes returned to the field immediately." The diary goes on to say that

Major Sailer led a force of twelve dive-bombers and seven Navy torpedo planes sent to locate and destroy this task force. Because of darkness and the weather they were forced to return after going only eighty miles. (It may be that the weather and darkness were the most fortunate thing that could have happened insofar as these pilots were concerned as the diary does not show any fighter coverage.)

Shortly after midnight, there were flashes of big guns, star shells, searchlights, fires, and explosions between Savo Island and the field, and it was evident that a major naval battle was taking place in the harbor. The Japanese had planned a repeat of the October shelling of the airfield and were bringing the Hiroshima Division (38th) to put it ashore near Koli Point in order to retake the field. In support of this operation, they had brought the division from its triumph at Singapore to Rabaul and had there loaded it on eleven large transports. These moved to the Shortland Islands at the southern tip of Bougainville, about 300 miles from Guadalcanal, to await the naval armada being assembled.

In support the Japanese Navy had assembled a task force of two battleships, nine cruisers, thirty-three destroyers, and two carriers. The carriers were protected by an additional four to eight destroyers. Despite the sighting by Hronek and Eck, Adm. Richard K. Turner (the admiral in command of the surface Navy in the area) did not believe there were any carriers in the area. In fact, the Japanese had about 215 operational aircraft in the area in addition to 48 on the *Hiyo* and 47 on the *Junyo* (the carriers sighted by Hronek and Eck).

To counter these forces we had two battleships, eight cruisers, twenty-two destroyers and one aircraft carrier. The carrier, *Enterprise,* had a total of seventy-eight aircraft, and at the Guadalcanal airfields there was a total of ninety-four aircraft: thirty-seven SBDs, forty-eight F4Fs, and nine TBFs. Each of the naval forces was divided in task groups of varying size, and obviously all did not participate in all of the actions occurring over the next three days.

The Japanese plan was to send the two battleships, the *Hiei* and the *Kirishima,* along with cruisers, *Nagara, Atago, Takao,* and *Sendai,* and a force of about twenty-two of the destroyers on the night of the twelfth to shell the airfield for a prolonged length of time. The battleships were again relying on the thin-skinned high explosive shell used in the October shelling. Fortunately for our Navy, their shell hoists were crammed with these projectiles. If challenged on the surface, they were counting on the cruisers and the destroyers to block any intruders. Each of the forces had good intelligence on the strength of the other and except for the late detachment of our battleships, it would have been a fairly even fight; however, neither of our battleships, the *South Dakota* nor the *Washington,* was in a position to be used. It is presumed that the Japanese assumed that our Navy would vacate the harbor at night, as was its custom. Halsey, however, was of a different disposition and sent to oppose these Japanese forces six of our cruisers, the *San Francisco, Pensacola, Portland, Helena, Juneau,* and *Atlanta,* with fourteen of the destroyers. Our battleships missed the engagement because the Navy staff in Noumea did not detach them to go to Guadalcanal until too late. Both sides kept their carriers out of range of each other and of the shore-based aircraft. In some cases Japanese aircraft from the carriers covered their troop transports, and the *Enterprise* released one each of its dive-bombing, torpedo, and fighter squadrons to operate from the fields at Guadalcanal during the later critical hours. Because the forward elevator of the *Enterprise,* damaged in the Battle of the Eastern Solomons on August 24, would not operate, after releasing those squadrons she withdrew to safer waters.

On Friday, November 13, the sun rose on the start of a day of beautiful weather that was to change as the day wore on. I was sent on a search with Kennedy and Sandretto of 141 at daylight. When we were airborne, we saw sinking and burning ships all over the harbor, eight in all. My first reaction was that we had sunk the entire Japanese Navy.

We saw the battleship *Hiei* slowly moving in a circle just north of Savo with an escorting destroyer nearby. There were four destroyers burning, three of ours and one of the Japanese, all of which I thought were the enemy. Two cruisers were immobile with major damage evident and another burning, all ours. As we watched, one of the crippled cruisers, the *Portland,* was firing at the *Yudachi,* the burning enemy destroyer. A round hit her magazine, producing such an explosion that she disintegrated and sank as we watched. We investigated the damaged Japanese battleship, *Hiei,* and she shot her antiaircraft guns at us so we pulled away. About twenty miles to the north of her, between Santa Isabel and Florida Islands, we saw another battleship and three destroyers steaming into the harbor at high speed. I thought that I was to have a grandstand seat at a fight between two battleships since it never occurred to me that one of their battleships would come into our harbor in broad daylight. We flew toward them and flashed our recognition signals with the thought that we could act as spotters for their guns. All of the ships promptly shot at us, and we withdrew and again sent recognition signals and flew on a parallel course so they would know that we had no intention of attacking. Again they shot at us. Realizing that these were not ours, but theirs, we first tried to call the radio control at Cactus to report the new situation, but we could not raise them. For the first and only time during the war, I had Chuck Showalter, my rearseat gunner, put out a trailing wire antenna and sent in Morse code the sighting report, to no avail. We then decided that it was of sufficient importance to call off any further search, and we returned and rushed to operations to report. Major Searles, the group operations officer at the time, informed us that they knew of the Japanese force, that it consisted of four destroyers, that there were more important targets, and that if we did not get out of there and finish our search all sorts of unpleasant things would happen. We took off again and completed the Santa Isabel search. By the time we returned, the *Kirishima,* the battleship which had been coming in from the north, and the destroyers were on a northward course away from the harbor. Morison's *History of United States Naval Operations,* Volume V, *The Struggle for Guadalcanal,* reports that a PBY sighted the battleship about ninety miles north of Guadalcanal later in the day.

Attacks started on the crippled battleship *Hiei* as soon as the planes could be armed. She was about twenty-five miles from the airfield. When Kennedy, Sandretto, and I had finished our search, I was sent out to lead my first bombing attack. By that time there was very little antiaircraft fire, and the *Hiei* was dead in the water. I remember that she was so big that when I made the final adjustment through my sight, the ship almost covered the entire 50-mil ring. Jug Herlihy, who was following me down, confirmed a hit. Later the weather became worse and when I was sent on another attack on the ship—this one led by Major Robertshaw—I was unable to complete it. On this flight and under these conditions both Knapp and Sandretto of VMSB 141 were lost. Others from our squadron made attacks on the battleship, and hits were credited to several of them.

The night battle of the twelfth/thirteenth was a disaster for our Navy but a blessing to us for the Navy had frustrated the Japanese battleships' attempt to shell the field. The Japanese had sunk the *Atlanta* and the destroyers *Cushing, Laffey, Barton,* and *Monssen.* In addition, the *Portland* was so badly damaged that she was out of the war for about two years. The *Juneau,* damaged in the night battle, was lost the next day while she was attempting to return to Espiritu Santo. The *San Francisco* was seriously damaged but was repaired at Pearl Harbor. The Japanese losses in addition to the battleship were two destroyers. Survivors of the *Atlanta,* brought to the airfield for evacuation, told us that the *Atlanta* was repeatedly shelled by the *San Francisco.* Subsequent events lend credence to the story. Dye from the shells of the *San Francisco* was on the deck of the *Atlanta.* (It is claimed that this was caused by the depression of the guns of the *San Francisco* in an effort to hit the *Hiei*, which was so close.) Valiant efforts were made to save the *Atlanta* throughout the day. She was pulled to the beach just off the airfield and her antiaircraft batteries shot down a Betty during the day, but she was finally scuttled. The *Hiei* was still afloat when darkness came but had settled lower and lower in the water. All of her light antiaircraft guns had been knocked out of action by the repeated bombings. The forward main battery was hanging over the side. During the night she was scuttled. History records that the transports with the troops left the Shortland Islands before dawn but when they learned the results of the battle, returned to the harbor. The first round of the fight was over.

I had the night standby at the field on the evening of Friday, November 13–14. The night standby consisted of six pilots who slept at the field to take any flights that arose during the night. Only Jug Herlihy and I were on night standby from our squadron. The remainder were from 141. Shortly after dark, Gen. Louis E. Woods, who had relieved General Geiger about a week before as the air commander, came by squadron operations and in a very dramatic fashion pointed to the map which was maintained there. He said something to the effect that there were twelve transports at the Shortlands with 30,000 troops (actually eleven transports with 12,500 troops) of the division which had taken Singapore and that by tomorrow morning they would be about 150 miles away on the way to Guadalcanal. He said that the Navy had done everything that it could do, that there was nothing between these troops and Guadalcanal except our dive-bombers, and that if we were unable to stop them the only question was whether an evacuation was possible. He ended by saying, "We lay the fate of Guadalcanal in your hands and know that each of you will do his best." For a second lieutenant who really thought that there was no question of winning, it was a very dramatic moment. At this time the dive-bombing squadron from the *Enterprise* had not been released to join us.

At about one o'clock in the morning we were awakened

by a sound like a freight train going overhead. We had all become used to the whistling, pulsating sound of bombs being dropped, and we usually had some warning. There were also the sounds of the aircraft engines. We had been shelled intermittently by Pistol Pete and were accustomed to his sounds. This was different. These sounds were followed by many explosions on the other side of the field. The 141 pilots who had been through the October shelling recognized the sound and promptly disappeared. I was sleeping in my flight suit, taking off only my shoes. I ran out of the tent in my stocking feet into deep mud. Jug said he was barefooted and in his underwear. Not knowing where to go, I decided that I was going to cut my feet on some of the trash, so I went back into the tent, put my muddy feet into my shoes, and went out to find a foxhole. By this time I had realized that we were being shelled. All of the foxholes around the night standby tent were filled to overflowing. Now either the ship fired a star shell or Washing Machine Charlie dropped a flare. The entire area became as light as day. I dove under a truck, but as I slid under in the mud, noticed that it was a gas truck and just kept going out the other side. In my mind's eye I could see the Jap admiral on the bridge watching me with his binoculars and telling the gunner to get me with the next round. I finally reached group operations, a dugout cut into a small hill. It was crowded. There was a squawk box from this dugout to another nearby, and over this came a question, "Are there any of the night standby pilots there?" If everyone there had not recognized me as a pilot because of my flight suit, I am not sure whether I would have spoken, but under the circumstances I had no choice but to answer, "Yes, Lt. McEniry, sir." The voice then asked were there any gunners and mechs there. Showalter was nowhere around and all of the others were total strangers. All denied being either a gunner or a mechanic. The voice then told me to wait there, that they would send a mech and a gunner, and that I should take off and attempt to attack the ships shelling us.

The shelling continued for what seemed about an hour

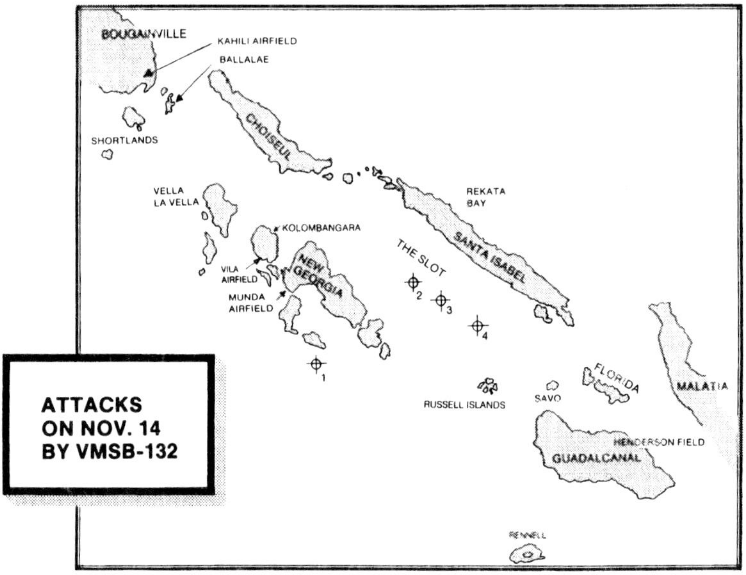

and a half. When it ceased, I finally went to the other dugout. Several of the planes had been hit and were burning, and the bombs on these planes were exploding. Whoever called had found more pressing business, and no one else seemed to know who it was. I was sent back to our operations to await any further instructions. I never found out who had called and I cannot but wonder what would have happened if I had been sent out. Most of the shells were falling across the field, hitting the fighter strip and the area where our pilots slept. One hit right in the middle of the officers' tents, but fortunately it was either a dud or an armor-piercing one. In the soft ground it made a hole large enough for a man to get into and so deep that it took a good flashlight to reach the bottom. In his diary Hap says that he slid into the hole to his armpits. Thinking it might be some kind of a delayed-action fused shell, at the first opportunity we quietly folded our tents and moved them to the other side of the hill where the other pilots were living, the old 141 area. The remaining pilots of that squadron were evacuated and sent home the next day. The records show that the field was shelled by the heavy cruisers *Suzuya* and *Maya* with more than 1,300 rounds of high-capacity eight-inch shells for about forty-five minutes, but I am sure anyone at the field will testify that it was more than twice that long. When the losses were counted, the dive-bombers had come through almost unscathed, with the loss of only one plane, while there had been seventeen planes of other designations destroyed and thirty-two damaged. We can only imagine how much greater the damage if the battleships of the previous night had been successful.

Morison says, "Back in Washington it was still the morning of Friday the Thirteenth. Everyone hoped that Callaghan's (the admiral commanding the task force of the previous night who had been killed) sacrifice had stopped the enemy; it was a shock to hear that heavy surface forces had broken through and were shelling Henderson Field. And when, a few hours later, word came that the Japanese transports were heading down the slot unopposed by surface forces, even President Roosevelt began to think that Guadalcanal might have to be evacuated. 'The tension that I felt at that time,' recalled Secretary Forrestal, 'was matched only by the tension that pervaded Washington the night before the landing in Normandy.' "

The searches took off at dawn and reports began to filter in. Our squadron diary reads: "On November fourteenth, Lt. Skinner [John Skinner, pilot] was ordered on a special search to determine the size and location of the enemy shipping. Twenty enemy ships were reported on a bearing of 330 degrees, distance 100 miles. Lt. Simpson reported negative from an anti-submarine patrol. Lt. Eck and Lt. Jackson from a sector search, reported an enemy task force of two battleships, one light cruiser and eleven destroyers bearing 300 degrees, distance 150 miles. This shipping was covered by an airforce composed of 6 Zeros. Lt. Hronek and Lt. Ball on a sector search reported two light cruisers and five destroyers on a bearing of 280 degrees. This report was followed in twenty minutes by a report of one aircraft carrier, two heavy cruisers and one battleship on a bearing of 300 degrees, distance 150 miles and with a speed of 15 knots. Lt. Kollman and Staff Sgt. Wallof on a sector search reported four large unidentified ships, bearing 210 degrees, distance 70 miles." While it is obvious that some of the ships that were reported were the same, and that the size and type of the ships reported were in error in many cases, there were enough to go around. In addition, one large convoy, consisting of eleven transports and a number of cruisers and destroyers, to this point unreported, was en route from Bougainville and the Shortlands with the Japanese troops.

The number of attacks and hits and by whom they were made will never be known with precision. The day was one of takeoff, attack, return, reload, and repeat. No one knew for sure who went on what attack. Many of us flew with the Navy squadron and with ten pilots of VMSB-142, who had been sent up the day before from Espiritu with the remaining planes from the *Hornet*. Without question, the first attack of the day took off about 0630 to locate the offenders of the night before, who had been reported about 170 miles away and south of New Georgia. This attack was led by Major Sailer and included Major Robertshaw and Lieutenants Kelly, Bright, Skinner, and me. I was flying wing on Major Sailer. Tex Kelly was on the other wing. We located the task force south of Rendova in the New Georgia group. Major Sailer led us in with Kelly following and me in the third position. Major and Kelly each got a hit, and I thought I had a hit also. My diary says that the major hit the bow, Tex Kelly hit the bridge, and I hit the stern and that antiaircraft fire followed us for eight minutes after the pull-out. Since I did not get a hit but only a near-miss, I am sure that the eight-minute figure was an exaggeration also. The memory of the cigarette when we were out of the antiaircraft fire and on the way back is still with me. When we landed, Major Sailer said to me, "Mac, you didn't quite get a hit. Let's try again." He scratched the first two pilots and placed my name and his as first on the next attack group.

(It is of interest that these ships which conducted the shelling were later attacked by the *Enterprise* dive-bombers on their flight to the Canal. They reported two of the ships were burning prior to their attack. The *Kinugasa* was sunk, the *Isuzu* badly damaged, and the *Choaki* and the *Maya* slightly damaged. All were cruisers operating out of the shelling group.)

When we landed the transports had been sighted. We rearmed and went on the second attack of the day. This time there were Sailer, Robertshaw, Kelly, Herlihy, Kollman, Hronek, Master Sergeant Gordon, and I from 132 together with pilots from other squadrons, making a total of seventeen SBDs. We took off and proceeded in the direction of Bougainville for about 150 miles when we sighted the largest convoy of ships any of us had ever seen. In my diary I have reported that there were twenty-eight ships. The squadron diary lists twelve transports, two light cruisers, and eight or nine destroyers. Admiral Tanaka, who was in command of this force, reported that there were eleven high-speed transports but he does not enumerate the escorting ships. His article stated that six transports were sunk, another one was damaged so badly that it returned to the Shortlands, and four reached Guadalcanal the next day. But more of them later.

On this second attack I was again on Major Sailer's wing, flying the only SBD-2 at the field. The difference between the SBD-2 and the SBD-3 was in the hydraulic system. In the -2 you had to slow down to open the dive brakes whereas in the -3s they would open at any speed. Since this transport group was covered on the outside by the cruisers and destroyers, we were picked up by the antiaircraft fire long before reaching the transports, and very naturally the approach and attack were made at a high rate of speed. When the major put us in the dive and opened his dive brakes, I opened mine, but since they would not open completely

I passed the major and completed my dive first. Again, I missed. The antiaircraft fire was intense, but we did not lose a single plane.

When we landed, Major Sailer said to me, "You missed again, Mac; let's go back and try again," and went to the flight board where the next attack was listed. He again erased the name of the flight leader and placed his name and mine as first and second pilots. On this third attack, the squadron diary reports Major Sailer, Major Robertshaw, Herlihy, Kollman, Simpson, Kelly, Skinner, Gordon, and me. Again we found the transports in much the same position but in disarray. Destroyers were laying smoke screens and were all through the formation of the transports. We made another high-speed approach and dove on the transports, and this time I made sure that I would get a hit. When we returned major said, "You got a beautiful hit, Mac. Now that we know how, let's go again," and went to the operations board. Again he erased the top two names, replacing them with mine and his. The squadron diary does not record this last attack. It is understandable in all of the confusion of that day, but this third attack on the transports was the one that will always remain in my memory.

In the beginning, the formation of Japanese ships had been very orderly, four columns of transports covered on the front and rear by destroyers skittering around much like water bugs. On each side was a cruiser and more destroyers. Following each attack by the dive-bombers, the formation became more confused. Ships were burning and sinking, and the destroyers became more enmeshed with the transports, some of which were burning and abandoned, giving the destroyers the additional duty of picking up the survivors and laying smoke screens to confuse the torpedo planes. By this time, the dive-bomber squadron and torpedo squadron from the *Enterprise* had joined in the action.

There were at least six of us on this last flight. On that day I never went on an attack with less than that number of planes. I do not know who they were because it is not recorded in the squadron diary. The transports were covered by fighters from Kahili Airfield on Bougainville and by planes from the carrier *Hiyo* (despite the fact that Admiral Turner never recognized the sightings of Hronek and Eck of the prior day). Morison reports that it was to the north but was never located but that it did furnish fighter coverage for the transports. On some of the attacks there were a great many Japanese fighters and at other times there were none. On this occasion there were enough to go around. They attacked us before we reached the ships so that we were under constant harassment even before we neared the antiaircraft fire of the ships. Our fighter cover had been greatly limited by the results of the shelling of the night before. On none of these flights would we have more than six to eight fighters to cover all of the dive-bombers, and on some of them there was no cover.

On this occasion, prior to reaching the ships, a Zero made a high side run on us and then made a run from below. On the first pass, he shot the triggers off both Showalter's guns and the cover plate off of one of them. On his low side run he shot away my engine-driven fuel pump so that in order for the engine to run I had to operate the auxiliary (hand) pump. Turning back at this point because of the damage to the plane was out of the question. The only protection for an SBD was the company of others for the mutual support of their rear guns. We dived on the first transport available. Since we had come in from the left-hand side of the transport force and entered the dive in a right turn, we were to rendezvous on the same side as soon as we could get out of antiaircraft fire. This would mean continuing a right-hand turn after the pull-out. Coming out of the dive, I looked to the right and saw Zeros waiting for us in that area and made an almost fatal mistake. I turned left, thinking that I was crippled, would be of no help to others, and that I might get home by myself if I could get through the ships and slip away.

As soon as I had committed myself I realized my mistake, but it was too late. By this time I had lost the speed that we had coming out of the dive, and the others in the flight had completed their runs and were going in the opposite direction. At that point I was irrevocably committed to continuing the course I had selected. Between a safe area and me were two transports, a number of destroyers, and a cruiser. The SBD, at full throttle, had a maximum speed of about 150 to 160 knots. I was right down on the water, lower than the deck of the ships, and the only aircraft in the very middle of the entire fleet. It was still necessary for me to operate the manual fuel pump to keep the engine running.

The first ship I approached was a big transport absolutely full of troops. They were all over the decks, running around, shooting their rifles at me. My front .50s were operating and I was firing at the ship, adding to the confusion of the troops. I came to it, pulled up, and went over it and on to the next one, another transport. As I was approaching this one, a dive-bomber from another attack (I later learned that it was a 142 pilot) released his bomb. I saw the bomb leave the plane and watched its flight until it hit the ship. All firing at me from this ship stopped at that instant. The bomb hit about twenty-five to fifty feet from the bow. The entire bow broke off and fell into the water. I passed over this transport and went on to the next in line, which was a cruiser. None of the Japanese reports of the battle indicate that there were any cruisers escorting the transports, a result of all the confusion among the Japanese. I can testify that there was a cruiser. She shot her main battery at me more than once. When the shells hit the water, they caused a big geyser to erupt. I flew around at least one of these on the way toward her and another after I passed. I did not fly directly over this ship since it was not in my flight path. There were still two destroyers who could shoot at me, but they were not close enough together to reach me with their light antiaircraft guns. They fired their larger guns but none exploded close enough to cause me any great concern. Showalter and I finally reached a point outside of all of the antiaircraft, and I gave a sigh of relief but through the intercom Showalter pointed out two Zeros maneuvering for a run on us. He had already told me that his guns would not operate, and I said something to the effect that we were in deep trouble if he could not get them to work.

I remained as close to the water as possible. The Zeros maneuvered into a position, one on either side and slightly above. They each started their runs. As they turned and reached the firing position, I started a turn toward one of them so that only one of them would have a shot at me. This had the effect of giving the remaining one an almost no-deflection shot. The Zeros had two 7.7 mms (slightly larger than a .30 caliber) which fired from the fuselage and two 20-mm cannons in the wings. I believe this Zero's 7.7s were entirely tracers. They seemed all over us. When he had us lined up with the 7.7 he fired his 20-mm cannon. It is a miracle that we were not shot down on that first run. Part of the Plexiglass over our heads was shot out. My instrument panel was hit and the distilled water that is a part of some of the instruments ran onto my flight suit. Another of the 7.7s hit the heel of my shoe, knocking my foot off the rudder pedal. Several of the 20 mms went into the radio which was located between Showalter and me, completely destroying it. There was no chance for any further communication between us. The pilot of that Zero was at the top of his class in gunnery. I promised myself that he would never get a chance to shoot at us again.

They both pulled up and made one or two more runs, but I made certain that the other Zero was always the one with the no-deflection shot. The pilot of the second was evidently just out of flight school and should have failed gunnery. I don't believe that he ever hit us. While this was going on I heard one of our rear guns fire. I didn't understand, but it was too late for explanations. By this time the Zeros knew they had a cripple, and the runs were as close as possible. I would have recognized the pilots if I had seen them again. On the next run, Showalter let them get right in on us and fired one of his guns. The Zero pulled straight up, fell off on a wing, and crashed in the water. With that, the remaining Zero flew alongside of us, did a loop, and left. The squadron diary reports that Showalter damaged an enemy plane despite ordnance difficulty. Showalter had reached inside the gun, found the broken trigger, and fired by depressing it.

We were still about 75 to 100 miles from home and the fuel pump was not working. I pumped for a while and finally climbed to about 1,000 feet and quit pumping. The hand-operated fuel pump was like the windshield wipers on an old car. It operated so that either the pilot or the gunner could pump. It was standard operating procedure for Showalter to operate the pump if the engine quit. He started to pump and very quickly found the engine would run only when the manual pump was being operated. He pumped until we landed. When we reached Savo Island, about 20 miles from the field, the oil pressure gauge started to fluctuate, indicating that we were about to lose oil pressure. By this time we were where rescue was assured, but landing an SBD in the water was no pleasure. The gunsight was a cast-iron pipe located in such a way that unless you were both cautious and lucky you could lose several front teeth and do considerable damage to your face. (Later models had electric sights and shoulder straps which did away with this hazard.) The oil pressure continued to fluctuate and then drop until by the time we reached the field it had reached zero. As I made the approach and cut the throttle, the propeller came to an abrupt halt. The engine had frozen from lack of oil. They pushed the plane off the runway. (When we examined it the next day, the armor plating protecting the pilot had several 7.7s and parts of the explosive 20 mms stuck in it.) It was getting dark and I remember thinking from the cot that night that if there were many more days like this one, I might not make it. Never before nor after did I have the slightest doubt that I would come back.

Admiral Tanaka says in his article, "In six attacks this day, the enemy had sent more than 100 planes. These had sunk six transports with bombs and torpedoes, killing a total of about 400 men. Amazingly, some 5,000 of the embarked troops and crews had been rescued by destroyers." I do not know how he could know of the troops and crew losses in all of the confusion. By the end of the day, the largest of the transports were sunk or burning and only the four smallest were still afloat. He goes on to say, "In detail the picture is now vague, but the general effect in my mind of bombs wobbling down from the high-flying B-17s, of carrier bombers roaring toward targets as though to plunge into the water, releasing bombs and pulling out barely in time; each miss sending up towering columns of mist and spray; every hit raising clouds of smoke and fire as transports burst into flame and then the sickening list that spells their doom. Attackers depart, smoke screens lift and reveal the tragic scene of men jumping overboard from burning ships. Ships regroup each time the enemy withdrew, but precious time was wasted and the advance delayed. But the four remaining transports, escorted by *Hayashio* and three ships of DesDiv 15, still steamed doggedly and boldly toward Guadalcanal."

At the end of the day, Admiral Tanaka still had four transports (the *Yamaura Maru,* the *Kinugawa Maru,* the *Yamatsuki Maru,* and the *Hirotrawa Maru*) and his destroyers which had rescued the troops from the sinking transports. His article indicates that he had assigned seven of his destroyers for that purpose. The enemy was still determined to place these troops ashore in accordance with the original plan, and he proceeded toward the island. By mid-afternoon one of the Japanese search planes had reported the presence of four of our cruisers and four destroyers in the waters east of Guadalcanal. To counter any interference with the unloading, the Japanese sent the battleship *Kirishima,* the heavy cruisers *Atago* and *Takao,* two light cruisers, and a destroyer squadron. By this time our two battleships, the *South Dakota* and the *Washington,* had arrived with four destroyers. The result was a naval battle in which the enemy lost another battleship while we lost three additional destroyers. There were numerous

The four Japanese troop ships beached in the Doma Cove area of Guadalcanal on the morning of November 15 and bombed by VMSB-132 as they reached the shore. One can be identified as the *Yamatsuki Maru.*

hits on each of the other ships, but none of them was sunk. During this engagement, Admiral Tanaka took his transports away from the island to await the results.

It had been planned for the remaining transports to reach Guadalcanal at midnight, to unload for two hours, and return to the Shortlands. The delay caused by this naval engagement had now made this impossible and in order to accomplish his mission, Tanaka requested permission to run the transports aground. This was denied by the immediate command but was granted by the overall command in Rabaul. The transports approached the coast in the early light of dawn and the four were simultaneously run aground. Our first attack on these took off at dawn. In order to get enough altitude to make a bombing attack, it was necessary to fly away from the field for about fifteen minutes. We returned still climbing until we reached the ships which were in the process of unloading. My diary says that I "hit right by it or on it—must have killed hundreds." The squadron made two attacks on these ships, leaving them burning wrecks. Morison reports that only 2,000 troops were put ashore.

After the first attack on the beached transports, Jug Herlihy and I were sent on the Santa Isabel search and found four cruisers and nine destroyers leaving the area. We flew too close to them, receiving some of the most accurate antiaircraft fire we had encountered, and it wounded Jug's gunner. Since they were leaving, group operations decided to let them go and sent us on to complete the search. In my diary I noted how mad Jug was that they would not send an attack out on them. I can't understand it today.

The big effort was over. Our squadron diary gives credit to various ones of the squadron for hits on the battleship on November 13, three hits on cruisers and seven hits on the transports on the fourteenth, and hits on the beached transports on the fifteenth. We all flew until we were exhausted. Showalter's log book shows that we flew more than twelve hours on the four attacks on the fourteenth. This was typical of all of us. The ground crews worked just as hard. There were the Navy squadrons, dive-bombing and torpedo, that flew into the field to operate and, of course, none of these was able to bring any of their support personnel so that the duty of gassing, arming, repairing, and reloading these extra planes fell to the lot of those exhausted ground support crews who had been on the Canal since early October.

After the battle was over, President Roosevelt is recorded as saying, "It would seem that the turning point in the war has been reached." Never again would the Japanese engage in an offensive operation. One of their captured documents read: "It must be said that the success or failure in recapturing Guadalcanal Island and the vital naval battle related to it, is the fork in the road which leads to victory for them or for us." To reflect on our inadequate training, equipment, and support makes the results of these days seem more unreal. But we did do the job.

★ 8 ★

Remainder of the First Tour

From November sixteenth until the twenty-seventh there were only the routine patrols and other such missions, and we were given some time off from the constant flying and standby that we had been subjected to for the first two weeks. The remaining pilots of our squadron who had not been sent up and the remaining 142 pilots all arrived. Our ground echelon arrived on November 26, to the relief of the overworked 141 ground echelon. Things were slowly improving.

After the battle of November 13–14, the Japanese never committed any large task force to the Guadalcanal area. Their efforts were now concentrated on the supply and resupply of the forces that were on the Canal. In the main, this was done with fast destroyers that left the Shortlands so that they would reach the limit of the dive-bomber's range just at sunset.

On November 30, the Navy decided to intercept these destroyers and sent a task force of five cruisers, the *Minneapolis, New Orleans, Pensacola, Northampton,* and *Honolulu,* together with six destroyers. Information had been received from a coastwatcher in the Shortland Islands that eight destroyers had left there, presumably on their way to Guadalcanal. Six of the enemy ships were being used as transports of men and matériel, and two were to act as guards. Through a series of unfortunate circumstances, in the battle that ensued, our Navy endured another disastrous defeat. The Japanese sank the *Northampton* and seriously damaged all of the other cruisers with the exception of the *Honolulu.* On shore we could see the reflections of the gun flashes and flares but were in the dark as to what was going on until morning, when the searches found the three crippled cruisers trying to get to the harbor at Tulagi. The *New Orleans* had lost 120 feet of her bow, the *Pensacola* was still burning, and the *Minneapolis* could barely keep underway. They were each out of the war for about a year. The Japanese lost one destroyer. The rest were out of our range by daylight. Morison, when reviewing this battle, writes, "It is always some consolation to reflect that the enemy who defeats you is really good, and Rear Admiral Tanaka was better than that—he was superb."

We attacked destroyers making supply runs on December 1, 4, 7, and 11. In each of these attacks, as in the prior ones on the ships, we took off and rendezvoused just off the field and proceeded climbing up the slot. This was an area between the islands of Vella Lavella, Kolombangara, New Georgia, and the Russells on the southwest, and Choiseul and Santa Isabel on the northeast. It extended from the Shortlands to Guadalcanal, a distance of about 300 miles. This route was the same one the transports had taken in the November battle. After the rendezvous we climbed to about 12,000 feet en route among the towering cumulus clouds customary in the afternoon. These same clouds covered the destroyers and generally the first thing we could see, just as dusk was rising out of the water, was the wake of one or more of the destroyers. Contrary to popular belief, darkness does not settle on the earth but rather rises from the earth. On sighting the wakes, the flight leader tried to ascertain the number of ships and get the formation in position for the attack. Since there were always at least nine, and on occasions as many as fourteen ships, it was our practice to try to make runs on as many of them as possible, and in many instances, if there were no enemy fighters, most of us dived on separate ships. The ships looked like toys frantically maneuvering on a peaceful sea. As we started in our dives, the destroyers would break their formation and commence abrupt turns at about forty knots (almost forty-five miles per hour). This, together with clouds and the wind blowing at the surface, made them most difficult targets. On several of the attacks the ships had fighter cover from one of several fields which the Japanese had constructed at Kahili and the Shortlands or from the seaplane base at Rekata Bay on Santa Isabel. The fighter coverage was seldom aggressive. It usually consisted of the Zero or a float biplane, lightly armed though highly maneuverable.

The antiaircraft from the destroyers was intense and accurate. It commenced some two or three minutes before we began our approach. The heavies (about five-inch) would burst with the familiar black smoke and follow as we approached. In order to avoid them as much as possible, the flight constantly changed its altitude and direction. The Japanese at this time did not have the proximity fuse, which exploded when it passed near a plane, so that their gunners had to set their fuses to explode at our altitude. Because of the time lag between the setting of the fuse, loading the guns, and firing them, they had to project our position about ten seconds from the firing. Our changes in direction and altitude complicated their problem. Most of us did not have any great concern with the heavy antiaircraft and worried more about some individual who did not know how to set the fuse or aim the gun. He was the dangerous one, even though several of these heavies might explode close enough to be heard or to rock the planes. I remember one of the 5-inchers exploding right in front of me just as I entered my dive so that I saw the flash and felt a hard jolt. I was sure that some major damage was done to the plane, but after landing I could find no evidence of it.

Light antiaircraft was a different matter. The volume of this was unbelievable. Until our first attack at about dark, none of us had any understanding of its volume. This type of antiaircraft was 40mm, 20mm, and the 7.7s. In the daylight it was not particularly noticeable until it had passed. Since we were not interested in shells that had passed, we seldom saw it. But on these dusk attacks we could see it as it slowly approached and suddenly passed.

We all had a great respect for it. It began at about 6,000 feet and multiplied in intensity until the pull-out. In the dive there was nothing that could be done about it except to hope, for we were so busy making the final corrections we could not take any evasive action. After the pull-out, we all constantly changed altitude and direction until out of range. We did lose at least two pilots and their gunners to antiaircraft fire, Joe Rohrl to ship AA and Robert McArdle to ground AA. Both were hit in their dives.

On December 1, late in the afternoon, a small Japanese task force was reported to the east of the Canal. Major Sailer led a nine-plane attack, but darkness intervened, and since we were unable to find the ships, we returned to Cactus after dark, still carrying our bombs. It was the first time any of us had landed at night carrying a thousand-pounder. Hap Simpson came in to land, forgot to lower his wheels, and landed on his bomb, skidding along the Marston matting with sparks flying. His gunner's reaction was, "Mr. Simpson, if that bomb had gone off it would have killed you." This, naturally, interrupted the landing sequence. It was Capt. W. F. Spang's second flight at the Canal, his first night flight in the SBD, and his first time to land with a bomb. In making his approach, he flew into the palm trees at the end of the runway and was killed.

On December 7 Major Sailer was relieved as commanding officer of the squadron and was made executive officer of the base. Major Robertshaw was to lead the afternoon strike and the afternoon search reported eleven destroyers in the slot on the way to Guadalcanal. Just as Major Robertshaw began the briefing, Major Sailer came in and told us that he had been relieved but that he would lead this attack. He erased Robertshaw's name as the flight leader and, substituting his own, took the plane assigned to Robertshaw. It was to be a nine-plane flight with Charlie Kollman leading the second section and me leading the third. For some reason, one of the major's wingmen did not get off, one of Charlie's had to return to base, and one of mine did not get off. I sent Don Herrick, who was to fly wing on me up to the major's wing, and I moved to fly wing on Charlie. The six of us proceeded up the slot, and at about dusk we found the nine Japanese destroyers in three columns heading for Guadalcanal. The major led his section on the destroyers in the first column, Simpson following and Herrick third. Charlie, for some reason, wanted to look the formation over and led us in on the third column, flying over the rest of the ships. Because of the light we could see the winking of the antiaircraft guns and the tracers slowly floating up to pass at a suddenly accelerating speed as they reached our altitude. After our pull-out, we saw a plane in trouble with Zeros making runs on it. Hap was the closest and said that he went by him because the major's dive brakes would not close. Hap was frantically trying to turn back and help. The major calmly called on the radio and said that his dive brakes would not close and that he was going to try to make a water landing near New Georgia. All of us were trying to get to him when a float plane made a head-on run and evidently hit him as he rolled over and hit the water. The SBD would not fly with the dive brakes open and he simply could not do anything to protect himself. Since he had gone on the flight at the last minute, his regular rear-seat gunner was not flying with him. Whether or not this contributed to his death none of us knew, but we had become accustomed to flying as a team and we all wondered if Staff Sergeant Stanley, his regular gunner, could have helped. We all felt a real sense of loss.

On December 11 another flight, led by Major Robertshaw, was sent to attack some destroyers. Lt. Joe Rohrl did not pull out of his dive. It was his first attack, and he had told us that it was the day his wife was expecting twins.

In a night attack on December 16 Frank Christian was lost. Ball, C. L. Bright, P. H. Kellogg, and Marvel were all evacuated for different reasons during the first part of December.

Some two or three days after the November battles, we were given our first time off. There were no showers or provisions to bathe available, and we were all still wearing the same clothes and flight gear we had worn since we arrived. The weather in that part of the world is unusual. During the days it probably reached at least 100 degrees and at night we slept in sleeping bags. It rained almost every day, and all of the foxholes had mud or water in them. The area outside of them was either muddy or dusty. We were awakened at about 3:30 A.M. and taken back to our tents after dark. We were as filthy as it was possible to be. The Lunga River was just off the southwestern end of the runway. It was a beautiful, swift, rocky stream coming out of the mountains and jungle behind the field. We all went to the tents and found some clean underwear and socks and headed for the river, determined to get our first bath. As we approached the river we came upon a patrol of ground Marines with their rifles at the ready, creeping along the trail. Very naturally, we asked them what they were looking for. They reported to us that someone at the river had been shot by a sniper. They were trying to find him. We told them to follow us, and we would be their bait because we were going to take a bath. They did follow us, and I am happy to report that either the sniper had left or chose not to shoot because of our guards.

Some time in the latter part of November or the first part of December, I was given an artillery spotting hop for the front-line Marines. A Lieutenant Hawkins flew in my back seat and called the artillery in on some of the suspected enemy positions. After the hop was completed, we flew behind the lines and he shot at several Japanese with the 30-caliber machine guns in the rear seat. Several days later he came back, and we took a plane up and looked over an area that he was to patrol on that night, and again we hunted the enemy behind the front lines with the 30-caliber. Since I had been so accommodating to him, he asked me whether I would like to go on the patrol with him that night. I never considered myself adventurous, but I did want to see and learn everything that I could, and his invitation was an opportunity to learn something new, so I accepted. I arranged with Jack Sperzel, our operations

Second Lieutenant Hawkins in the rear seat of an SBD at Guadalcanal. Lieutenant Hawkins was posthumously awarded the Congressional Medal of Honor for action at Tarawa, and the airfield there was named in his honor. Each gun was 30-caliber and held 600 rounds.

officer, not to have an early search and collected a tommy gun and several grenades which I hung on my belt in a very professional manner. It never occurred to me to clear the patrol with Major Robertshaw or anyone else. Hawkins was to pick me up at operations before dark. I was there waiting for him when Major Robertshaw came up and saw me equipped for war. He asked what was going on, and I told him of the arrangements I had made with Hawkins. That was the end of my patrolling. The Major informed me in no uncertain terms that I was not going on any such mission, that we were trained as pilots, and that was our job; furthermore, I probably would give the patrol away and get some of them killed. When Hawkins arrived, I gave him my grenades and told him the sad news. The next morning Hawkins came to the field to tell me that the patrol had located some Japanese, had waited until daylight, and had wiped them out without any member of the patrol even being wounded. Hawkins was later one of the real heroes at Tarawa, where he was awarded the Congressional Medal of Honor, and the airfield on Tarawa was named Hawkins Field in his honor.

On about November 25 I was sent to try to bomb Pistol Pete, who was still shooting at the field intermittently. It was arranged by the coastwatcher that one of the natives was to place a smoke pot near the gun at exactly noon and the pilot was to give him time to get away and then to bomb the smoke. I was on station for about two hours, but no smoke. No one at the field knew why the foul-up but I later met the coastwatcher, Martin Clemens, in Australia and mentioned it to him. The best explanation we could rationalize was that there had been a mixup in the dates since, he said, the native had placed the smoke and no one bombed it. I believed that the Raiders subsequently sent out a patrol which silenced the gun.

The missions, subsequent to November 15, were somewhat varied in nature. We furnished antisubmarine escort for ships damaged in the naval battles: the cruisers, *Pensacola, New Orleans, Portland, Minneapolis,* and *Juneau,* and the destroyer, *Meade.* After the *Juneau* was out of our range and we no longer furnished the escort, she was torpedoed and sunk in one of the real tragedies of the time. Her escorting ships left, thinking that her sinking had been reported when in fact it had not. Almost all of her crew were lost, including the five Sullivan brothers, whose loss simultaneously was a famous World War II news story. When it was finally discovered that she was lost, we searched in vain for the survivors. In addition, we ran the regular sector searches, and on almost every one for several days after the battle there was a report of survivors in lifeboats or on some of the other islands. We were never told whether those we were able to report were rescued.

Beginning on November 17, intelligence became interested in the Lambetti plantation located at Munda Point on New Georgia. That search was asked to investigate the area and to check for anything unusual. Cecot and I reported from one of these that all of the native villages of the area were deserted. We were finally told that the Japanese were building an airfield in the area, and beginning about November 23 a daily mission was sent to bomb the area. On December 15, the Japanese put the field into operation. They had built it under the coconut trees, and when the surfacing was completed, the trees were blown out and a truckload of coral was dumped in each hole.

Munda lay only 180 miles northwest of Guadalcanal. It could become a real threat to operations there. The Japanese had obviously made a serious error in not building the field in the early days, but they were sure that they would retake Guadalcanal, and it would not be necessary. They based planes at Munda only intermittently, but we never knew when they would be there. On one flight in December, operations decided to bomb it with six B-17s. The antiaircraft fire from Munda was heavy and six of us were to accompany the B-17s to bomb the antiaircraft guns. The only fighters accompanying the mission were to be Army Air Force P-38s, which had recently arrived. I went to the joint briefing. The B-17s were to go in at 20,000 feet and the P-38s were to be above them. A P-38 was a very fine fighter when operating at high altitude but was not effective at low altitude. We were to go in at 12,000 feet for our dive-bombing run and after the run would be at sea level. After an extensive briefing by the Army Air Force, I asked where our fighter cover would be because there were to be no Marine planes except the six of us. The P-38 commander emphatically said that he was not coming down to cover us no matter what. This seemed to embarrass the Air Corps brass until the B-17 commander said that if we were jumped he would bring the 17s down and for us to get under their wings. We did not see any enemy fighters and the 17 commander called me after the mission to thank us for a good job of flak suppression. In my diary I noted that six B-17s can create a lot of damage.

By the middle of December we were all absolutely worn out. We had flown from daylight to dark. The food, if there was any that anyone could eat, was terrible. In his diary Hap says that we were not fed anything except soup made out of K-rations for three days. Jug's notes to me said that we had nothing but onion sandwiches for three days. My diary for December 15, after describing an attack on Munda, is as follows: "As we started back my motor quit. I called Chuck Kollman and told him it had quit and I was going in for a water landing. He started down with me and it caught back up. I don't know why it quit or why it started again. I was as calm as could be. In fact, there was a sigh of relief. I'm tired and disgusted. Yesterday afternoon Chuck and I went on the Malatia search. It surely is a pretty island. There is the place where I would like to go down. When I got back I found that Kellogg had piled in at the end of the runway near the trees. He caught fire on take-off. When he piled in, some Army boys pulled him out. He was knocked out. His head all cut up. They saved his life because his plane burned to a crisp. Vitkis, his gunner, got out O.K. Paul is in bad shape. Had to have a transfusion. He was pretty badly burned also. I think he will go back to the States. He's lucky to be alive.

"We are all in one Helluva shape. Out of the 28 pilots we started with we have 15 left. All of those 15 have worked until they are in a bad way. The colonels in charge of this place are to blame. They are the two biggest SOB's in the world. We are working our heads off and they do nothing but bitch. The food is awful. Yet they keep us here. Kelly looks like a ghost. He's lost 40 pounds. If they don't do something quick we are all going to be lost. Then to top it all off, I didn't make 1st Lieutenant. Something messed up. I'm in a terrible mood." I might say that I did make first lieutenant. Someone in the group missed my name on the promotion list, and when Major Robertshaw went to check, they found their mistake.

By this time, according to Showalter's log book (mine was lost later during the war), he and I had flown forty-one flights of varying kinds, for a total of one hundred hours in a period of thirty days. Of this total, thirteen were dive-bombing attacks, nine on shipping, and four on ground targets. The remainder were searches, antisub patrols, artillery spotting, message drops, and the like. Most of the others who had come up to Cactus in the early days had comparable time. I had taught Showalter to fly, and on the antisub patrols he would fly the plane from the back seat. On several such occasions I almost went to sleep. On almost every night Washing Machine Charlie was over the field dropping flares and bombs. Many times Kollman, Janson, and I, having got into our foxhole and gone to sleep while the raid was in progress, slept in the hole for the rest of the night. All of us were tangled with each other when the watch came to wake us for the early morning searches. We all had to go to the field even though we were not scheduled for a search. Of the fifteen pilots still able to fly, ten of us had been there since before the big battle and only Kelly, of the first four, was still alive. Kelly had an ear infection. It was so bad that the entire side of his head was swollen out of shape. He continued to fly the searches and antisub patrols. We were living on black coffee, bread, and a thin soup made from K-rations. Few of us could get a cup of coffee to his mouth with only one hand. All of us were physically and mentally exhausted. We were all making mistakes in our flying that could be disastrous. Malaria and jaundice had grounded several.

Pilot fatigue was a problem recognized as insidious as the war went on. Or, maybe, nothing could be done about it early in the war because there just were no replacements available. Lt. Comdr. LeRoy C. Simpler had been the CO of a Navy fighter squadron, VF-5, on the *Saratoga* but had operated his squadron at Guadalcanal after his carrier had been hit in one of the engagements. After being relieved and sent home he was interviewed at the Bureau of Aeronautics in Washington, and he commented on this problem. He said, "There's one fact which I believe is not properly understood, and that is pilot fatigue. A man's 'guts' is directly proportional to how rested he is—nothing more or less. With land-based operations in the combat zone, it is much harder to keep rested than it is on a carrier. I'd rather operate off a carrier for *two months* than from a good *stiff* land base for one week, because on a carrier you're either resting or you are not as far as a pilot is concerned. The carriers are very good to their pilots, give them every break, and don't heckle them with being at general quarters all the time. As a result you should get plenty of rest. But on land, with 'Cheerful Charlie' floating around and throwing a bomb every 45 minutes every time you get 'flemished down' and just about to drop off to sleep, it certainly wears the boys out! I think that about *5 days of intensive action* is about all a man can stand; with interims I think he can last three weeks. I had to evacuate pilots after three weeks for I felt that keeping them there longer would have seriously affected their future use to aviation." He went on to say, "One of the first manifestations of that [pilot fatigue] is a loss of weight—stomach trouble—shakes all of the time—chronically irritable. Every time a new outfit goes into action, their losses may be a little bit heavier at the beginning but their winnings are far in excess of what an older squadron would have that had been there for too long a time. . . . However, an experienced squadron, rested, will always pack a terrific wallop."

Maj. Joe Renner had served as operations officer of the group at Guadalcanal while we were there and later was the CO of a fighter squadron. In a Bureau of Aeronautics interview in July 1943, he said, "We became greatly fatigued because of the hours we had to fly. In the Guadalcanal area, at least, pilots have been required to fly too many hours a day. For a period of six days, one group of fighter pilots was flying an average of six and a half hours a day. The time they were not flying, they were on scramble stand by, which meant that they had to get up before daylight and either take the dawn patrol or the scramble stand by. . . . It doesn't take too long to burn the boys out at that clip."

December 17 was my last day to fly on this tour. In the

morning I led another routine bombing on Munda. At about four o'clock the major came and told me that they had heard that there were to be some Japanese ships at Munda and that I was to lead another flight back up there at 5:00 and get back after dark. My diary notes, "I went to group operations to try to get the story. After piddling there for about 45 minutes while Cooley [the group commander] got excited over the general being there, he told me that the attack was postponed until 9:30. It was my first dive-bombing hop at night. Nine of us took off, rendezvoused and started. Ran into bad weather a couple of times but reached our objective. When we got there, there was a rain squall right over where the ships were to be. I went into it and dropped a flare but it went out. Dropped another but couldn't find anything. We searched for about half an hour, when I decided to go home. Called all planes and told them to drop their bombs on the field and return to base individually. I went over and dropped my bomb and started back. When I got back, I found out that Jackson had found a ship, bombed it and hit it—there were supposed to be ten destroyers, but he only found one—he said that he had given up when he saw it. Christian is missing. He either dived in or got lost. Hope it is the latter." After this flight, Dr. R. J. Johnson grounded the five of us who had the most flight time.

Frank Christian was one of the pilots who did not arrive at Guadalcanal until after the battle. He and Andy Jackson had become close friends. They were the only two of us who showed any outward religious influence in their lives. They read the Bible together. We subsequently found out that Frank had been captured. We never knew whether he had bailed out or had landed in the water, but he was taken to Rabaul where, according to "Tokyo Rose," he had told the Japanese that MAG-14 was at Guadalcanal and that Colonel Cooley was the group commander and that he was from 132. Colonel Cooley was incensed that he had talked. Our reactions were that the Japanese surely knew that the group was there, and what difference did it make who was the group CO. We all said that if they put bamboo splinters under our fingernails and lit them (our idea of the kind of torture we would be subjected to) we would tell them anything they wanted to know. We felt we knew nothing that could be a secret to them. Andy showed the only real emotion that I remember any of us showing over the death or loss of one of us, despite the fact that as we grew to know one another, a close feeling grew among all of us. After the war, it was determined that Frank was put to death at Rabaul. At that time our instructions, if captured, were to give only our name, rank, and serial number. Later in the war, these instructions were changed, and we were told to give any false information that we could think of but to answer the questions put to us because the Japanese would lose face if we failed to, and this would lead to torture.

One other fact seemed of some importance to us later on. Of all the married pilots in the squadron, only Major Robertshaw survived. Captain Spang, Joe Rohrl, Frank Christian, and Andy Jackson were all killed. Joe Rohrl was killed the same day his twins were born. We all said that the ones who were married added 1,000 feet to the release height of the bomb and ten knots to their landing approach speed for their wives; in effect we were saying that they would not take the same chances because of their responsibilities. In retrospect, I am sure it was only a coincidence.

Curley Bright had been evacuated for yellow jaundice. It seemed as though candy was one of the things which would prevent jaundice. The Japanese parachuted some mints to their troops which fell inside our lines and Doctor Johnson was able to get them for us. They were in a big wooden box about as large as a footlocker in white paper sacks with Japanese writing on the outside. All of us except Major Robertshaw ate them as if they were going out of style. He refused to eat any of them because he told us that the Chinese used human excrement as fertilizer, and he didn't think they were edible. To the rest of us, this made absolutely no difference. Two or three days later, VMSB-233

Some of the pilots at Henderson Field in December 1942. In the background are the night standby tents. *Left to right: first row,* Christian, Kellogg, Herlihy, Simpson; *second row,* Eck, Kollman, McEniry, Wallof, Robertshaw, Cecot, Sperzel, Jackson.

Pilots at one of the foxholes. The ready tents are in the background. *Left to right:* Eck, Wallof, McEniry, Skinner, Christian, Kellogg.

Squadron members at Espiritu Santo in the New Hebrides Islands, our rear area where the squadron reformed after each of its tours of duty at Guadalcanal. *Left to right:* McEniry, Kollman, Simpson, and Janson.

was sent in to relieve us. They had come straight from the States and were all hale and hearty with their clean flight suits and fresh haircuts, while we looked as though we were jungle rats in our dirty, muddy and torn flight suits and no haircuts since September. They were immediately interested in the Jap mints though they did not know what they were.

Everyone, upon reaching the tropics, simply must open a dried coconut and drink the milk and eat some coconut meat. It is a fine laxative and as a result, everyone had diarrhea after being there for a little while. We were jealous of our mints. They were our reward for all that we had been through, and we did not intend to share them with anyone. When one of the 233 pilots asked what they were, someone in the squadron (I think it was Russ Janson) said they were a laxative and that after you ate the chow here for a while you would become so constipated that you would have to take laxatives regularly to avoid serious constipation problems. For two or three days no one from 233 ate any of our mints. Finally one of them said that no one could take that many laxatives, and the secret was out. By then we had eaten or hidden most of the mints.

We were evacuated on December 24 and sent back to Espiritu Santo for reorganization. On December 26 we were given one week of rest and relaxation ("rack and ruin") in Sydney, after which we returned to Espiritu.

★ 9 ★

Sydney and More Combat

When we left Guadalcanal, we were given a blood test to determine whether we were carriers of malaria. Those of us who were not, about eight of us, were sent to Australia for a week of rest. We were first flown to New Caledonia for one night and then were put on a DC-3 for the eight- to ten-hour flight to Sydney. Upon arrival we all went to the Australia Hotel, the most modern one, and asked for rooms. None of us had had a haircut for about three months, we were in our dirty flight suits, and we probably scared the desk clerk. When he said they had no rooms, we asked where we might find some, and he suggested a small hotel just across the street. We went over there and were given rooms, but without baths. We bathed, shaved, put on clean clothes, and walked back across the street and were allowed to register. All of us went to the barber shop in the hotel for the works: haircuts, shaves, mud packs, manicures, everything they had.

Sydney was a great place to go at that time. Australians thought the Marines had saved them, and nothing was too good for us, the first Marines to be sent there. The people welcomed us with open arms. We went to a big cricket match and the spectators applauded when we came in and insisted that we have tea with the teams in their dressing-rooms at half time.

After our experiences of the past two months the food in Australia was beyond our expectations. It had one major drawback. There was rationing. Under their system we could spend only a limited amount of money on a meal. In the beginning we solved this problem by eating one meal and then going to another table in the restaurant and ordering another. This was not satisfactory since the dessert seemed to end the meal. The second solution worked better. Four of us would ask for a table for eight and then order for our friends and when they failed to show, would eat their meal so it would not go to waste. The desserts, such as pie for one of us and ice cream for another, worked better.

On one occasion, an Australian lieutenant asked me if I would buy him a drink in the hotel bar. I was happy to do so, and we spent some time in the bar together. It turned out that only residents of the hotel could buy at the hotel bar. At the end of the day, we had become such friends that I gave him the Marine emblem off my hat and he gave me his off his Australian hat. The next day I saw his picture on the front page of the paper. He had been awarded the Victoria Cross, the equivalent of our Medal of Honor, for his actions at Crete or Cypress.

After we had been there for six days, Chuck Kollman came in and said that he had met some American Red Cross girls who had just arrived from the States and that we were all to go to a big party that night. It was to be our last night because we were to go back to Espiritu the next morning. Everyone in the squadron and the Red Cross girls went to Prince's, a nightclub just across the street. We stayed there until they closed, went back to our hotel, packed our bags, and sat on the curb in front of the hotel with all of the Red Cross girls to await the truck which would take us to the plane for return. While sitting on the curb, a milk truck drove up and we bought all the milk we could drink, and kissed the girls good-bye. My date on this occasion, though it was hardly a date, was my wife eleven months later after we both came home.

Our squadron was sent to Guadalcanal two more times and after each tour of duty was sent to Sydney for rest and recreation. Each time we were less welcome. More and more troops were sent there on R and R and I am afraid that we were not very pleasant guests. We all had more money than the local people and after being where we couldn't buy anything, spending money was fun. The second time in Sydney, I was not able to get in touch with Marjorie of the Red Cross. She was in Brisbane and out in the country with the 155th Station Hospital which supported the 32nd Army division in New Guinea. The third time, however, I was able through the Sydney office of the Red Cross to get word to her, and she came down. When I asked her to marry me, she suggested that I go home, see how things looked, and let her know. As soon as I reached Bessemer, I sent a cable that said it looked the same here as there and to please come home. I was able to pull the wool over her eyes, and she did come home, and we were married on the west coast just before I was sent out on my second tour overseas.

Our second and third tours of duty at Guadalcanal, one in March 1943, of about four weeks, and a second in July and August 1943, of about eight weeks, were relatively quiet ones.

On the second tour we were merely holding while the gains of Guadalcanal were consolidated. We flew occasional bombing missions to either the airfields at Munda in the New Georgias or to Villa on Kolombangara or to Rekata Bay, the sea plane base on Santa Isabel. These Japanese bases were operational but were used by the Nips only occasionally. There were some bombing raids on us at night but nothing of consequence. I noted in my diary that one of these raids hit three B-17s, all of which were loaded with bombs, and the fires and the explosions of their bombs and machine gun ammo made quite a show for a long period of time. Most of our flights were the usual searches and antisub patrols. On one of these patrols, I was assigned the Florida Island and the harbor patrol and saw nothing. Tex Kelley and an enlisted pilot named Ballard from another squadron had the patrol that covered the Russell Islands, just to the north of Guadalcanal, where we were building a new fighter strip. The Japanese sent a dive-bombing attack on this facility along with a number of Zeros as cover. The Zeros caught Tex and Ballard. Tex had the presence of mind to go to the PT boat facility, and their

Officers of VMSB-132 after the reorganization following the first tour of duty. *Left to right: front row,* Kollman, Janson, Herlihy, Jackson, Gordon, Jones, McGuckin, Beneke; *second row,* Wallof, Dieffenbach, McArdle, Caldwell, Robertshaw, Rupp, McDermott, Skinner, Hicks; *third row,* Lewis, Hughes, Dr. Stevens, Sperzel, Simpson, Roberts, McAllister, Pope; *back row,* Mullen, Cohron, Cecot, Blaine, Stock, Kelly, McEniry.

antiaircraft guns were able to cover him until the Zeros left. Ballard flew back to Guadalcanal, and two of them shot him full of holes on his way back. He was the most "shook" man I have ever seen. His gunner was wounded and he was shaking so badly that he could not get the drink of brandy they gave him to his mouth. I saw nothing, but resolved to keep a better watch in the future. The main value of this tour for us was to break in our replacement pilots and to show them the general area. We left after about a month and returned to Espiritu Santo, followed by a week in Sydney and more training.

During the rest period at Espiritu we lost Jackson and his gunner on a simulated attack on some cruisers. One of the fighters ran into him, and they and the fighter went into the water. The *Louisville,* one of the cruisers, went over to the place in the water where he hit and I flew over it and by my Aldis lamp (the device whereby we could signal ships) sent a message asking whether there were any survivors. The *Louisville* came up on the radio and asked what I wanted to know. I then asked my question by radio and they replied in the negative. We also lost a TBF on the same problem when, for some reason, a wing came off the plane as it was making an attack. On the plane as an observer was Bill Shields, the wing intelligence officer and a good friend. It was an expensive mission to be only a training hop.

We also lost Walt Eck, Bill Hronek, Ken Gordon, and Howard Hicks during the time we were at Espiritu. Walt Eck tried to do some acrobatics at too low an altitude and flew into the jungle. He and Bill Hronek had been the closest of friends. They were classmates in flight school and had been together ever since. They had owned the Cord automobile together. Hronek tried to show a group of the Raiders who were also stationed on Espiritu how to locate the crash site but flew too low and crashed into the jungle himself and was killed. Gordon and Hicks were lost searching for the crew of a big bomber lost at sea. We had been assigned a sector to search in an effort to find them. The weather was bad and there was a strong wind. Gordon and Hicks missed the island on return, and by the time the radar found them and gave them a vector to base, it was dark and they were short of fuel. They came into the island from the north but did not have enough gas to reach the field. They decided to attempt to land in the water. A night water landing was hazardous at best. They dropped some float lights to assist, but Hicks evidently was knocked unconscious on landing. His gunner was able to get out and was later rescued. Gordon, in making his approach to land in the water, hit some trees and was killed. His gunner lived, though when he was rescued he was badly injured.

When we left Guadalcanal, we had lost both Major Sailer and Captain Spang. Except for Major Robertshaw all of the rest of us were only lieutenants. A squadron normally had two majors and several captains. All of our replacements were lieutenants. In addition, it was normal to relieve a squadron commander after one or two tours in combat, and his replacement should have had some experience in combat if possible. We heard that we were to get a new executive officer, a Major Boyington, the "Pappy" of subsequent fame. He came down to the squadron and said that he wasn't any "damn" dive-bomber and made deprecating statements in general about dive-bombers. We were proud of our accomplishment. We thought that we had had to carry the dirty end of the stick and do the hardest job, and it didn't set well with any of us to hear anybody running us down. We felt that if things got too tough, fighters could get out of it, but there was no way for us to run away from anything at any time. For whatever reason, his orders were never issued or were cancelled, and he remained in the group pilot pool.

During the time we were in the rest camp, they put shoulder harnesses in the SBDs so that if you cracked up while landing or taking off, you would have a better chance of living, much like those in today's automobiles. They were uncomfortable and none of us would wear them. The group finally put an enlisted man at the end of the runway to take the name of any pilot who was not wearing his harness and he would have to report to the CO. Then we put the harness on for takeoff and took it off as soon as we were airborne. Finally, when one of the pilots in another squadron had to make a water landing and did not cut his face or lose any teeth because he had been wearing his harness, they had no more trouble with any of us.

Our third and last tour was of more interest than the second. VMSB-142, the other dive-bombing squadron in our group, was sent back to the States and we were held to assist in the taking and securing of Munda by ground troops. We were told that they specifically wanted our squadron because of our experience, so during the last week in June, we were sent back up to Guadalcanal. It was a different place. In addition to taxi ways and revetments for the planes, the field had been widened and lengthened. Our quarters were near the beach and in quonset huts. We were fed in a mess hall rather than out of our mess gear. The food was good. There was a quonset hut for a ready room and for operations. There were even running water showers.

Our mission on this tour was primarily in support of the troops which had landed and were attempting to take the field. The operation was much more difficult than had been planned and took much longer than was expected. By this time, there was a Navy squadron with the responsibility for all of the antisub and searches. Our flights were all bombing hops and we had one almost every day. They were usually on Japanese living areas and heavy gun positions. On several we supported a Marine Raider Battalion that had been landed on the opposite side of the island to interdict replacements and supplies meant for the enemy front lines. They had quite a problem, and we tried to assist them. Close air support, as it was known later, was in its infancy, and our main concern on this kind of a flight was not to bomb our own troops. We were to bomb in an area that from the air looked like a jungle with no markings on the front lines. These attacks caused me some concern because as the flight leader, my bomb was going to mark the area where the others would bomb. Fortunately we never dropped on our own, but I am sure with better markings we could have done more damage to the enemy.

On one of these hops we lost Hunky McArdle, one of the replacement pilots, and his gunner to antiaircraft fire, which was at times heavy and accurate. Several of us came back with holes in our planes. At one time Charlie flew his plane back with a hole through his wing large enough to stand in. His main problem was control of the plane because of the hole. The most interesting of the flights on this tour were the one to Kahili on Bougainville and the one described in accounts by John Stock and Jug Herlihy, quoted in Chapter 11.

Excerpts from Hap's diary show typical times during this last tour:

> July 13th: Up at 5:15. Had a strike at Munda. After I released my bomb on the field at about 1,500 ft. I went on down as low as 400 ft. strafing all the way. The place really looks a mess with all the bomb holes in it. We all returned safely. Time of the hop 3 hrs. 45 min.
>
> July 14th: Up at 8 AM. Went down to Strike Command and had a lecture on the new IFF. [This was a system for the radar to identify a plane, friend or foe.] We have a strike at Villa at 12 noon today. We took off at 1300. We went up there but could not bomb the field because of the bad weather. We had to come around a big front and did not arrive until 1730. My flaps would not open so I had to land without them. My hydraulic system was broken. I landed with 10 gallons of gas because of such a long hop. Time 4 hrs. 40 min.
>
> July 15th: Went on another strike to Bairoko harbor on New Georgia. I went in Roberts' place on this strike because he wasn't around when it was called. I led the second section in Herlihy's division. After we dropped

our bombs in the designated area we strafed a Jap barge that was in the harbor. More fun!!

July 16th: Up at 3:45. Had shipping standby at the field all day. No activity. We are to go to Bougainville tomorrow to bomb shipping at Kahili. It's very tough up there because of such heavy AA and the Zeros. Hope I get to write in this again. At night we had an alert. Washing Machine Charlie came over and dropped his bombs at Koli Point after circling us for about five minutes. I heard he killed six men and wounded some when he dropped his bomb. He came over again at 1 AM but I don't know where he dropped this time.

July 17th: Up at 4:30. Took off for Bougainville at 6:40 AM. Arrived there at 9:35 AM. This strike included 36 SBDs, 76 fighters, and 36 TBFs. As we arrived at the Shortland Is. about 20 miles from Kahili Air Field, we saw about 10 or 12 ships in the harbor. Our division dived on a cruiser or large destroyer, we aren't sure. Roberts and I got direct hits on it and it sank a few minutes later. We were not bothered by AA because the Japs had their Zeros up. I saw about 5 Zeros but they did not make any runs on me. However, a few fellows in our squadron returned with holes in their planes from the Zeros. Skinner had his wingtip shot off but he was able to get back safely. The only SBD lost was a Navy boy. He was shot down by a Zero. One TBF was shot down and lost and we lost six fighters but two of these six pilots are probably safe. The Japs lost 51 Zeros, which makes our losses pretty light. They lost the cruiser and about 6 destroyers and some small boats, thus making the strike a success. We returned to Henderson Field at 12:15. The total distance of this hop is over 600 miles by round trip. At night about 8:00 Washing Machine Charlie came over and stayed in the area until midnight causing us to lose precious sleep. Our AA guns shot thousands of rounds at them and our fighters chased them with no results. I do not know where they dropped their bombs. Evidently all this was to harass us and it did to some extent. [This is the same flight that is mentioned in the next chapter, where the numbers of planes differ. The numbers in Chapter 10 are correct.]

July 18th: Slept until 8:30 AM. We went to Strike Command and were briefed for a strike on a small island inhabited with Jap troops near Munda. Left on the strike at 1300 and dropped bombs and returned at 1630. We all hit our target which about demolished the island.

We were kept at Guadalcanal until August 2 because it had taken much longer to take Munda than was expected. When the airfield was secured we were relieved.

After Munda was taken we went back to Espiritu and some of us went to Sydney for our third trip there. While the others were waiting to get to go to Sydney, they received orders back to the United States on a freight boat. In a day or two after we returned, we were given our orders home and we went aboard the escort carrier *Suwanee,* which was carrying all of the enlisted personnel from VMSB-141 to San Francisco.

⋆ 10 ⋆

War Stories That Improve with Age

In the early part of our tour, radio facilities throughout the entire South Pacific area were nonexistent insofar as aircraft were concerned. For obvious reasons there were no radio navigation facilities like radio beams, a standard in the continental United States. There was no radio control of aircraft traffic at any of the fields from which we operated. About the first of December, Joe Rohrl, one of the pilots in our squadron at Guadalcanal, constructed a control tower consisting of four palm trees with a platform at the top, about fifty feet in the air, and a field telephone connected to the squadron operations tent and to group operations. Prior to that time there was nothing to serve as a tower. In order to operate the telephone, we had to turn a crank on the side to make the phone ring at the other end. Traffic around the field was controlled by an Aldis lamp which sent a red or green light to notify an aircraft in the traffic pattern whether it was cleared to land or should circle for any reason. The tower was manned during the daylight hours by one of the pilots, with an enlisted man to assist. Tower duty was considered most distasteful because, in the main, of boredom. Nobody wanted the duty, and it was generally manned by a pilot who had been grounded for some physical reason or other. In addition, the tower had a Very pistol which could shoot a red or green flare much like a Roman candle to indicate that the field was open or closed or to warn a pilot approaching the field who had failed to see the red Aldis lamp.

Paul Kellogg, one of the original pilots who went out with the squadron on the *Lurline,* was unlucky enough not to arrive at Guadalcanal until after the November battle. His home was in Philadelphia, but he had gone to the University of Tennessee on a basketball scholarship. His uncle had owned a small circus and in the summers Paul had worked as a barker at the carnival. He could give the entire spiel of the barker. He was a typical Philadelphia Irishman with the dry wit that is associated with them. Shortly after he arrived at Cactus, he drew tower duty for some period of time, and while he was on duty, squadron operations received word of an air raid on the way. The notice of an air raid was generally by a phone call from group to squadron operations. Shortly thereafter an artillery shell-casing was hit two times with a hammer to notify everyone of the impending condition red (enemy planes were coming over), but before that it was customary for our operations to notify the tower duty personnel so they could get down out of the tower. I was at operations on this occasion and was asked to notify Paul. I rang the phone and he very efficiently responded, "Tower, Lieutenant Kellogg, sir." I realized he didn't know who was calling or what was about to transpire, and it occurred to me that we could have a good time with him, so on the spur of the moment I said, "This is Colonel (unintelligible) and we are about to have an air raid."

"Yes, sir."

"This raid is going to be a big one and intelligence must know the number and types of the planes."

"Yes, sir."

"We think that they will come in low to strafe and to bomb the field and it is important that we know their tactics. We want to get the side numbers off the planes so that we can identify the units from which the planes come. It is very important. You must stay in the tower. Do you understand?"

"Yes, sir."

I hung the phone up and stood by to answer. Almost

immediately it rang. Kellogg said, "Who is this?" I answered, "Mac." He said, "Mac, some damn colonel just called and said that there was to be an air raid." "Yeah, Paul, and it is supposed to be a big one. There is something different about this one but we can't find out about it here." He said, "I know. There are a lot of planes coming down and they are supposed to strafe the field."

"You had better get out of the tower and into the foxhole at the tower."

"I can't. This damn colonel has told me to stay up here and count the planes and identify the types. He even wanted me to get the side numbers for some of those fools in intelligence."

"Can you read Japanese?"

"Hell no."

"I don't know why they would want you to stay in the tower. You know that you are sitting right on the bull's eye? If you were strafing a field, wouldn't you shoot at the tower?"

"Sure. But I got to obey the orders. What would you do, Mac?"

"Why don't you get the man in the tower to get a rope and when it gets too hot for you, you can slide down the rope and get into the hole."

"Sounds like the best thing I can do."

Shortly thereafter, the enlisted man from the tower was at operations looking for a rope. We told him about the joke and kept him there for the rest of the time. They rang the artillery shell-casing, and we went out to watch the air raid. When we could see the planes, and the antiaircraft guns had started, I called Paul and told him what I'd done and to get out of the tower. He vowed to get even with me and I am sure that he would have, but shortly thereafter his engine quit on takeoff and he piled in at the end of the runway and was burned severely. After months of recuperation and with the help of some friendly doctors, he was returned to flight duty and was finally given a commission in the regular Marine Corps.

John Skinner had the tower duty during the latter part of December, just prior to our being relieved. There were no traffic rules. You were supposed to land into the wind, but if there were no wind or if the wind were directly across the field, aircraft landed in either direction. Normally, planes landed and took off toward the ocean, but most of the big planes, B-17s and the like, were not stationed there, and the landing being, in many cases, the pilot's first there, he would not know the pattern. Skin was in the tower about the middle of the morning. He looked to his right and saw a P-38 making his approach to the field and on his left was the ocean. A B-17 was making an approach from the opposite direction. He gave each of them a red light with the Aldis lamp. Both continued their approaches. He took the Very pistol and shot a red flare out over the landing strip. Both planes continued their approach. As quickly as possible, he reloaded the Very pistol and fired another red flare. Neither waivered from its approach, and both touched down at the same time on opposite ends of the field. He reloaded the Very pistol for the third time about when the planes met in the middle of the field, and at the last second the 38 pulled up over the 17, jumped over it, and as I remember it continued its landing pattern. (This may be my imagination. Skinner tells me he does not remember.) Skin promptly shot himself in the middle of his hand with the Very pistol. He still carries the powder and a round circle in the middle of his palm where the aluminum end of the charge in the Very pistol hit him. I had to relieve him in the tower. Doc Johnson had grounded me for "pilot fatigue." I still haven't forgiven Skin.

Except for Major Sailer, Charlie Kollman was recognized as the best dive-bomber in the squadron. He had reported to the Naval Air Station at San Diego shortly after all of the Marine pilots there had been sent to Midway and was able to complete the entire ACTG dive-bombing syllabus. In addition, Charlie was a natural. Nothing seemed to worry him. He was a completely "happy-go-lucky" individual. He and I were sent out together to the Marshall

McEniry and Kollman on the wing of an SBD.

Islands for our second overseas tour of duty. I was stationed at Headquarters Marine Corps in Washington when he came back, and I was able to get Chuck sent to the Naval Aircraft Test Facility at Patuxent, Maryland, as a test pilot. He was given the AD, a new Douglas dive-bomber, as his aircraft to test for production, and he did an outstanding job. When a congressional committee went to Patuxent for a demonstration, Charlie was the one who put on the show for them.

Charlie and I flew a number of missions together. On the mission on December 7, Major Sailer led a nine-plane flight. Charlie led the second section of three planes and I, the third. When three of the planes did not make the rendezvous, I flew wing on Charlie. It was late in the day when we first saw nine Japanese destroyers. As usual, they were in three columns with three ships in each column. They were on a supply mission, planning to arrive about midnight, land the reinforcements and supplies, and be out of range by daylight. As we were preparing for the attack, the light was such that we could see all of the antiaircraft fire as it came up in the dusk. The air looked full of lightning bugs. The major led his section in on the lead ship in the column to our left, and Charlie led us over the entire squadron of destroyers before deciding which ship he was to take. When he finally dived, he and his first wingman took the first ship in the third column and I took the following one. Charlie hit his amidships, I hit alongside mine, and as I pulled out of the dive, I could see Charlie's burning fiercely and sinking fast. By the time I had passed Charlie's, it sank and, as a burning ship does, the smoke and fire came off the water with an absolutely flat bottom as the ship goes under the water. He was the only one of us who ever sank a destroyer. I don't know of any other dive-bomber who did, though I am sure others have. It was quite a feat to hit a destroyer. As an example, on the day following the sinking of the four carriers at Midway, the same Navy dive-bombing squadrons located and attacked a lone destroyer. Fifty-eight dive-bombers attacked without a single hit. Near misses may sink a destroyer or may cause it to return to base as the intelligence reports indicate many did from missions such as these, but a direct hit with a thousand-pounder will surely sink one. None of the intelligence reports have credited Charlie with this sinking, but I know he did it. General Vandegrift presented Charlie with a beautiful Japanese sword for doing the most damage to the Japanese fleet. He was awarded the Navy Cross also.

Charlie and I went on several searches together. On one of these, as we returned to the field, Charlie motioned me to come in as close as I could get. He kept motioning me to get closer until just inches separated our planes. Intense concentration is required to fly that close, and I was, of necessity, watching him with all the intensity possible. Out of the corner of my eye I noticed the control tower at the field. We were only a few feet off the ground. I pulled up at the last second to miss the tower, and when we landed, I asked him if he was trying to fly me into the tower. He said, "No, just checking your reaction time."

Once, we returned late from a search and supper was over. The messmen had saved us some of the Vienna sausage that the others had. By the time we ate them, they were green and when we asked if they were green when the others ate them the messmen said, "Yes, sir." About fifteen minutes after we had finished, Charlie became violently ill. I was holding his head as he vomited when suddenly I became sick also. By the next morning we were as good as new. Charlie did get malaria more than anyone else. On one of our searches, I noticed that Charlie was not playing around but merely flying the search in a normal manner. I realized that this was not like him and when we landed, I found him having violent chills. Charlie was sent home after our second tour of duty at Guadalcanal because of his malaria.

On that night attack on Munda on December 17, described in Chapter 8, we were late returning, and only eight of us made it. Frank Christian had gone down. I was the last to land. Normally under these conditions all of the other pilots were in their beds. As I taxied in and got out of my plane, there was Charlie crying like a baby and when I asked what was the matter, he replied, "I thought you hadn't made it."

Hap Simpson was the youngest of all of us. He was reared in Round Hill, Virginia, and had attended Shepherd College for two years before deciding to join the flight program at Anacostia in October 1941. In flight school he was in the same class with Major Robertshaw. They finished flight school in August 1942, and reported to the squadron about the first of September. I believe that we would all agree that Hap was the most congenial, relaxed, and aptly named man in the squadron. I never knew him to do an unkind or ugly thing. He was absolutely dependable. After our first tour of duty, Hap flew on my wing for our remaining tours. We tried to get him to lead one of the divisions, but he always made the excuse that he had to take care of McEniry. In addition to all of his sterling attributes, he had the most marvelous power of concentration imaginable. On one occasion during our third tour at Cactus, we were briefed for a bombing mission to Munda. After the briefing, there were eighteen pilots and eighteen gunners in a ready room waiting for the trucks to take us to our aircraft. The ready room at that time was a quonset hut, and noise of everyone talking and the confusion of getting into the trucks and leaving was as would be expected. Hap was reading a novel. Thirty-five of us left, started seventeen airplanes, taxied out, and took off. Hap remained there reading his book until finally his gunner came back and told him that the flight was leaving. Happy rushed out, started his plane, took off, and caught us about halfway to the target. I was disgusted and tried to send him home, but he just smiled and stayed in his usual position. By the time we returned, all was forgiven.

Hap and I had flown together for so long that we could communicate with each other with hand signals. The radio in the SBD could be tuned to only one frequency, the bomber frequency. The fighters were on their own frequency; consequently, there was no communication between us and the fighters. There were occasions when communication between us was highly desirable so that we could know what the fighters were doing or what they saw. We decided on one such occasion that Hap would set his radio on the fighter frequency and that he would let me know what he heard by hand signals. We had perfect confidence in our ability to communicate. The flight was a bombing raid on the Japanese airfield at Munda or Villa. There were twelve to eighteen dive-bombers, and our fighter cover was to pick us up as we entered the Munda area. The sky was full of big cumulus clouds, and we were forced to fly around them so that we were a little late in arriving at the target. When we were about thirty to forty miles away, Hap began to give me some signals. They were entirely unintelligible. In addition, my radio was not working. I could not talk to anyone. Hap became more unintelligible and finally seemed to me to be almost frantic. I knew the message he had was important, but I had no idea what it was. I signaled to try to find out if for some reason the mission was recalled but could tell that this was not the message. Meanwhile I had led the flight in a large circle. Finally, I waved to him to forget it and went on in as planned. It was a routine strike, but when we landed I found that on the fighter frequency he had heard that there were about fifty Japanese fighters waiting for us over the target, and he was trying to tell me to circle until the fighter cover had run them off. Our delay in arriving had had the same effect for we did not see a single enemy plane. Hap informed me that he was never going on the fighter frequency again; that it was all right to go if you didn't know what was ahead, but he did not want to know and, particularly, be the only one who did.

On our third tour of duty at Guadalcanal, our commanding general was one of the old timers of the Marine Corps who had been much decorated in World War I. He was a kindly old man who shall remain nameless. He had a problem with alcohol and was later relieved as air commander at Okinawa. As the flight leader, I was called to a briefing on a task force consisting of a Japanese cruiser and three destroyers that had been in the Kula Gulf the night before. There had been a naval battle and the *Helena* had been sunk. I was given the briefing by Col. Kay Pottinger, the group operations officer, as to where I should search and what to expect. The general was there observing. After Colonel Pottinger had finished, the general went to the map on the wall and said something to the effect that if we did not find them where we had been briefed, we were to search up toward Bougainville and beyond, indicating the area on the map we were to search. It was far beyond the range of the SBD. I very respectfully told the general that if we went that distance none of us could get back to the field. He looked at me, obviously well into his cups, and said, "Who said anything about coming back?" As I left the briefing I asked Colonel Pottinger what I was to do. He merely said, "We know that you will take care of it, Mac."

Eighteen of us and eighteen TBFs took off. We first went

to the Kula Gulf area. As a result of the naval battle, a Japanese destroyer had run on a reef near Kolombangara Island. The task force we were hunting was not there. All of the pilots knew of the briefing. We started northeast in the direction of Bougainville, and at the limit of our range we had seen nothing. I called on the radio and suggested to Hap that maybe the ship that we had seen on the reef in Kula Gulf was the cruiser we were looking for. He readily agreed that he was sure it must be one of the ships. We turned back and all thirty-six of us made a run on the ship, blowing it out of the water. It did fire its antiaircraft guns at us so it was not a complete waste. When we returned, I had to go to group operations for a debriefing. The general was not there. I reported to Colonel Pottinger that I had made a real mess of the mission and had mistaken the destroyer for the cruiser and that by the time I recognized my mistake it was too late to stop the attack. Colonel Pottinger's only comment was, "Too bad." After the war it was determined that no Japanese cruisers were involved. The *Helena* was sunk by torpedos from the destroyers.

Between our second and third tours at the Canal we had been given two new captains, Russ Rupp and Dick Caldwell. Prior to going to the Canal for the third tour, both were promoted to major. They had both been instructing at the Naval Academy and had had little flight experience. It put both of them at a distinct disadvantage to come to our squadron under these circumstances, and they chose to fly wing on John Stock and me for the experience. They were both nice fellows, but it was hard on them trying to command where all of the pilots had more flight know-how than they. Caldwell flew on my right wing and Hap on my left. When we were sent to Guadalcanal for our third tour, Major Robertshaw had been moved to group operations officer at Espiritu. Rupp was our new CO and Caldwell our exec. One of Major Caldwell's problems was that he could never make the rendezvous after a dive. We all knew it was prudent to rendezvous as quickly as possible for protection from fighters, and I knew that Hap was the best in the business, so I always turned toward him on the entry so that he would be the first to pick up my turn. No one wanted to be alone for longer than necessary. Somehow Major Caldwell usually came back from the mission by himself, a practice not conducive to long life. After several missions and talking it over with Caldwell without any change on his part, Hap and I decided that I would dive toward Caldwell so that he would be the second in line and Hap would follow him and see what he did. We picked a safe mission, and I dove toward Caldwell's side and Hap followed him down. At the turn, Caldwell never made the rendezvous turn but merely continued in a straight line for several miles. As best we could determine, he wanted to get farther from the antiaircraft or perhaps was so fixated on getting away that he never saw the plane in front of him turn. Caldwell was never jumped by Zeros, but there were several occasions when we thought that he would surely get shot down. We never understood but marveled that he made it back every time.

Going over on the *Lurline,* each of us had a normal amount of concern as to how we would react to being shot at in anger. We wondered if we would turn tail and run, or what we would do. No one had ever tried to kill any of us. All of us, with the exception of two, kept these concerns to ourselves. One of these was Horatio Ball and the other was A. B. Marvel. Ball was a small man who could not wait to get there so that he could start sinking ships and killing Japs. He went to the Canal on November 7, but somehow he did not take part in any of the attacks until after the big fracas of November 12–14. I am now convinced that he must have arranged to be unavailable during that time of confusion, or, possibly the plane assigned to him on each occasion had something wrong with it, at least in his mind. He did fly some searches and antisub patrols. Some time after this period, he was assigned to fly an attack on one of Major Sailer's wings and I was on the other. As we approached the Japanese destroyers, the major moved us into an echelon so that I was looking down at the destroyers and over Ball and the major as we made the approach. Ball had his head out of the cockpit so that he could see everything as we approached. His neck was as long as a turkey gobbler. I was looking right over him and then over Major Sailer and at the destroyers. The first burst of heavy antiaircraft was just off our wing tip and so close that we could hear it explode. With the explosion, Ball dropped his head so that I could now see only the top of it. He must have crouched down and lowered his seat to its lowest position. The major pushed over into his dive, and we each followed. We were at about 12,000 feet. No sooner had we entered the dive (I was following Ball), than his bomb left the plane, and he turned for home. It must have been released at 10,000 feet. Ball never went on a bombing mission again. If he was put up for one, he went to the dentist or to sick bay for some complaint. I think he lost two or three teeth. Dr. Johnson finally sent him back to the rear area on December 12.

As for Marvel, he did not arrive until after the November battle. He was ready to go, but when he was put on the operations board for an attack, he became violently ill, and we could hear him retching all night long. The next morning he was too sick to fly. When he recovered and was put up for another attack, again we could hear him throwing up. We all thought that he was putting his finger down his throat so that he would not have to go. No love was lost on either of these men. Marvel was sent home for "fear of the dark." His flight orders were revoked. We never saw him again. After the war, Ball flew for Pan American as a captain.

Maj. Joe Sailer, our commanding officer when the squadron was formed, was from one of the main-line families of Philadelphia and graduated from Princeton with an engineering degree. He subsequently went to flight school, graduating from Pensacola in 1930. After a tour of duty as a reserve officer, he had a career with the Sperry Gyroscope Company, makers of the Norden bombsight and the automatic pilots in most of the early planes, including the SBD.

When we first joined the squadron, he gave the lecture on the use of the autopilot, and while at North Island at San Diego in my only flight in the squadron, I landed while flying wing on him and he made the landing using the automatic pilot.

Since most of us were not in the squadron for any length of time before leaving the States, we did not have any opportunity to get to know the major. He was a quiet, unassuming man, and appeared to be shy and retiring. As a flight leader he was superb, never hurried, never rattled, never excited, always calm, deliberate, and perfectly in charge in every situation. I had the opportunity to fly on his wing on many attacks and there was never any doubt that he was in charge in all respects and that we would be in the right place at the right time.

On one occasion I had the night standby at the field. On this duty you were to sleep at operations to be available for an emergency, usually to fly what were called "harassing flights." These flights were of about three hours' duration and were flown over the Japanese lines for the purpose of keeping them awake. You were loaded with one 500-pound bomb and two 100-pounders. This was the maximum for the bomb stations on the SBD. We always wondered who was the most harassed—they or we. The weather was questionable many times. The mountains rose to 8,000 feet just inland. There were no markings to indicate the front lines, and we certainly did not want to drop a bomb on our troops, so that the bombs were dropped well behind the enemy lines. On night standbys, Major Sailer usually came by operations. The weather on one particular night was lousy. It was pouring rain and the clouds were right on the ground. Our squadron operations had us standing by for an improvement in the weather. The phone from group operations rang, and group wanted to know why the night harassment hop had not taken off. Major took the phone and told the person on the other end that the weather was too bad. There was something said by group and the major said, "I'm sorry. The weather is too bad for me to fly and I certainly am not going to send any of my pilots out on a night like this." Then he turned to us and said, "All of the night harassing hops are canceled." And he walked out of the tent. We could have hugged him. That kind of leadership will get the most out of the men who fly for you. I believe he did. After his death, he was awarded the Navy Cross for his leadership and his accomplishments. He was credited with nine hits on ships in thirteen attacks—the best dive-bombing record of the war.

Maj. Ben Robertshaw was our executive officer when we left the States. He had been reared in Philadelphia and had been an outstanding athlete in high school. He had always wanted to go to Annapolis but was unable to get an appointment upon his graduation from high school in 1930. In order to try for the appointment, he went to Friends Central School in Philadelphia for another year, without gaining the appointment. As was typical of him later in his life, he was undeterred. He spent another year at Swansely School in Manassas, Virginia, and then received the appointment. At the Academy, he graduated with credit. While there, he was captain of the 1935 football team and was awarded a sword for personal excellence in athletics. Twenty-five years later, *Sports Illustrated* picked General Robertshaw as center on its "Silver Anniversary All American Team," a team composed of former football players who after this period of time had accomplished the most in life. (Bear Bryant of Alabama fame was an end on this same team.) No one could have been more deserving than Ben. Robertshaw. Under his command there was no way to do anything but the right way.

After graduation from the Academy, he was sent to China and assigned to the Sixth Marines. Here he commanded a machine gun platoon at Shanghai for only nine months before returning to San Diego for a year. During this tour in Shanghai, he served as mess officer and said that after that tour he never again complained about the chow. In San Diego he married, and a year later was again ordered to China for twenty months, this time to the Fourth Marines

Maj. Louis B. Robertshaw, the executive officer with a letter from home.

as commander of a rifle platoon protecting the International Settlement at Shanghai. Following this tour, he was sent to the Academy to serve as the plebe football and basketball coach until in February 1942, he was ordered to Pensacola for flight training. Upon completing it in August, he was ordered to the First Air Wing at North Island where he joined VMSB-132 and was promoted to major.

Robertshaw was largely responsible for whatever we may have done as a squadron. He furnished the leadership that was so necessary under the existing conditions. Two of our pilots were lost before most of us arrived. When Captain Spang was killed, none of us knew how to act. Should we hang our heads, be quiet, be remorseful? Most of us had only known the captain for a short period of time, and there was no great sense of personal loss. Robertshaw could see the dilemma. I remember his coming into the ready tent and saying that it was a loss for all of us, but that his death was for a good cause, that there would be other losses of friends who were close to us, and that while it was regrettable and we would miss them, there was a job to be done and it was up to each of us to do the best that we could for our country in whatever circumstances we found ourselves. The tension left. We all knew that it was now up to us to do our best. None of us ever really thought he himself would be killed, but we all wondered about the others.

While Major Sailer was alive, he led almost all of the attacks, and Robertshaw in most cases flew in either a wing position or leading the second section. The exec had less flight time than most of us, but his rank must have made him conscious that as the senior officer he would be expected to lead the flight. He acknowledged to himself that until he had some experience he might not have been the best one to lead. These facts made absolutely no difference to any of us, but because of his training and background, they were important to him. After the death of Major Sailer, he led every mission that he was on, but by that time he had experience and was a fine flight leader.

On one occasion, after the death of Major Sailer, I was leading the squadron on an attack. It was to be coordinated with a Navy squadron. We were briefed on the approach to the target by the group. The weather was foul and the mission could not be flown in the way we had been briefed. The Navy squadron returned to base, but we were able to get to the target, and it was clear. We hit the target as we had been instructed but had not been able to make the approach in accord with the briefing. When we landed, Robertshaw met me and said that the group CO wanted to see me. We went into the group office where I was given a dressing down for not flying the mission as instructed despite the weather. I knew enough not to say anything except, "Yes, sir." When we came out the major said to me, "Mac, the reason you are leading is because we have the confidence in you and your judgment. Once your wheels leave the deck, it is your mission and any way you fly it, I am behind you." As a lieutenant who had just been chewed out, I appreciated this confidence and backing.

Robertshaw was a winner in every sense of the word, and he didn't like to lose at anything, but the squadron, when it was in the rest area at Espiritu Santo, was divided into "Yankees and Southerners." We played volley ball, softball, and all sports as these teams. Those from the far west were on the side of the Yankees. Except for Robertshaw and Stock, few of the Yankees were inclined to athletics, and the Southerners won everything. We knew it irritated the major, and some of us, particularly Tex Kelly, took great pleasure in rubbing it in. While we were in Sydney on our rest leave, a meeting was held in the lobby of the Australia Hotel every morning at ten to make sure there was no trouble and to pass out any pertinent information. One morning Robertshaw gave each of us an address and said that we were to meet there at 2:00 P.M. that day. No explanation. When we arrived at the address, we found that it was an ice-skating rink, and the major announced that there was to be a hockey game. He had arranged for the rink to be ours with all of the equipment for an hour. It was the Yankees' turn to have a good time, because none of us from the South had ever before been on ice skates.

Sometime during the first trip to Sydney, Major Robertshaw told me to meet him at an oyster bar for some reason. When I came in, the waiter put in front of me a plate of oysters on the half shell that the major had ordered for me.

I thanked him but told him that I had never eaten a raw oyster and never expected to. He said they were good and I should try one. I again told him no thank you. He said, "Eat one." No one considered not doing anything that he said to do in that tone of voice. Accordingly, I took one of the oysters, put it in my mouth and swallowed it whole. He was watching me and said, "Chew the next one." I protested but followed his order and found out that they were not as I had imagined and ate all the rest.

Between our first and second tours, after we had received our replacements, the squadron was divided into halves for flying. On our second tour at the Canal, there was not much to do except fly searches and antisub patrols. Both of these were dull and boring flights, the searches taking about four and one-half hours, and our fannies just ate into the parachutes by the end of the flight. We were given very few attacks and most of these were on Munda, a milk run, but more exciting than the searches. I led one-half of the squadron and Major Robertshaw the other. We alternated days of flying searches and strikes. It was our day for strikes, and Robertshaw's half had returned from the morning searches when the group called and reported some Japanese ships on which an attack was to be sent out. I was briefing our half on the situation when Charlie Kollman, who led the second division in Robertshaw's half, persuaded the major that because we had had all of the attacks so far, he should make us take the afternoon searches, and they would take the attack. The major bought Charlie's idea and told me that our group would take the afternoon searches and that they would take the bombing mission. I protested. That was not the arrangement, I said, and we were supposed to take the attack. He told me that was not the way it was to be. I said something to the effect that I knew he was tough and that he had the rank, but that I had thought that he was fair. I can still see him as his neck turned first red and then white. If this had happened to me when I was a squadron commander, I would have transferred the lieutenant before the sun set. Not Robertshaw. He looked me up after all of the missions of the day were over, apologized to me, and said I could rest assured that it would never happen again.

During the latter part of May, while we were in the rest area, Major Robertshaw was relieved of the squadron and made the group operations officer. It was a hard time for all of us. Not only did we respect Major Robertshaw, but we thought him one of us, and we all felt indebted to him for his leadership. We were genuinely fond of him. He had set the tone for our operations and had made an indelible impression on us. This relationship, leadership, and example would continue for the rest of our lives. Russ Janson's diary explains best of all how we felt. "Sunday May 30. Major Robertshaw gave us his farewell speech at our lecture Friday. It didn't start as a speech but ended as such. He really felt bad—at times he just couldn't talk for 30 sec. He would just stand and try to say something but nothing would come out. Nobody had the heart to look at him or at anybody else. Everybody was examining their hands or just looking at the ground. The entire squadron's hearts went out to him. He hates his new job and wishes so much he could be with us—but I guess there's no hope. After he left no one moved, just stayed where they were until he was out of sight. Everyone hates to see him go." We were fortunate to have had him as a leader and our commanding officer.

Chuck Showalter was my gunner, a big rawboned boy from the hills of Tennessee, and a more loyal gunner no pilot ever had. We met on the ship going over when we were assigned to fly together. I never made a dive-bombing run that he did not report I had hit the target. The gunner faced backward and could see only where you had been, never what was coming. He rode down backward in the dive and could see what happened after the pull-out. I believed Showalter until the time I turned after a pull-out and saw that I had missed. When he said that I had hit, I told him that I had peeked and that I had missed. He said something to the effect that it was "right by it." In general,

Lt. Col. Charles E. Showalter, CO MCAS, Danang, Vietnam, briefing Lt. Gen. Victor Krulak, CG FMFPAC, Maj. Gen. Jeff Fields, CG 3rd Marine Division, and Maj. Gen. L. B. Robertshaw, CG, 1st Marine Air Wing. Lieutenant Colonel Showalter was the author's gunner and General Robertshaw, the executive officer of the squadron at Guadalcanal. (Official U.S. Marine Corps Photograph)

a gunner had the worst of it; if the pilot was hit, he was sure to go down. We all had the utmost respect for our gunners. During our first tour, Chuck acquired a five-pound tin of raisins and gave them to me. Our food was so sorry and so scanty, I believe the raisins kept me going.

Relationships between pilots and their gunners were what you might expect. I didn't know a pilot who didn't think that his gunner was the best in the business, and who did not go to bat for him whenever there were promotions to be given. Chuck was a corporal when we left the States and had been promoted to tech sergeant by the time he was sent home. All of the pilots would go to see the major for their gunners when the time for promotions arrived. Gunners were just as loyal to their pilots and would reward them whenever they had the opportunity. They also had the know-how and the daring to take chances that we never knew of. Somehow, a gunner would get an apple pie that was intended for the brass and bring it to his pilot. One time, mysteriously, we ended up with a case of beer. Walt Eck's gunner gave it to Walt, and no questions were asked.

They were the ultimate thieves. After the war, Chuck told me of some of their escapades. There was a supply dump two or three miles away from us near the beach. The gunners frequently got a weapons carrier after dark and drove near the dump. One or more of them engaged the guards in a conversation regarding flying while one of the others slipped into the dump and pilfered anything that looked good. One night, Chuck was the one to get in the dump, and he was able to get two large ten-gallon tins. It was dark and he couldn't see what was in them. Something scared off the others, and they returned to our camp in the weapons carrier without him. He struggled with the two tins through the bushes, finally reaching camp at about dawn only to discover that the tins contained Crisco. It turned out that Vitkis, Kellogg's gunner, knew how to make doughnuts and the next night all of the pilots were treated to doughnuts. They were very special treats.

We never had the opportunity to get to know the other enlisted men in our squadron very well. Our tours to Guadalcanal did not coincide with theirs because theirs were of different lengths, and when we were on the island we operated with the enlisted ground personnel from a different squadron in most cases. When we were at Espiritu Santo, our ground personnel might be at Guadalcanal, and at about the time that they returned we would be sent back up. When we were sent home we brought the enlisted personnel from 141 with us, and our enlisted and our ground personnel had to stay for another three months.

The parachutes of that day were not adjustable and there was not a parachute for each of us; each seat of each plane had one, and they were kept in the plane. Chuck and I were both big, which meant that we needed a plane with two large parachutes. Many times when we arrived at our plane (and the planes were spread all over forty acres), there would be only one and, on some occasions, no large parachutes in the plane. In these instances, you simply buckled the chest strap and took off, ignoring the leg straps if they were too small to hitch. At other times it was impossible to buckle any of the straps. On one strike we were struggling with our parachutes and Chuck, by accident, pulled the D-ring and the parachute spilled out on the ground. I am afraid that I was not the most patient man in the world, and I disgustedly told him to get the guns out of the plane, that I would fly without a gunner. Instead of that, he strapped himself into the plane without a parachute, and we flew the mission. I never flew a more uncomfortable mission. I knew that regardless of what happened, I would have to ride the plane down.

I never flew a bombing mission without Showalter, and I don't believe he ever flew without me until our third tour. Since Major Sailer was not flying with his regular gunner when he was shot down, a superstition had arisen that you would not get back unless you had your regular gunner. I had encouraged Showalter to apply for flight training, and toward the end of our last tour he was accepted. We were both as excited as possible when his orders back to the States for flight training arrived. On the morning that he was to leave, our squadron was given the mission of leading the first dive-bombing attack on Kahili Airfield on Bougainville. Since it was beyond our range, they hung wing tanks on the planes for additional gas. Our squadron was leading thirty-six dive-bombers and thirty-six torpedo planes to hit some shipping in the harbor. It was to be the largest bombing flight of the Pacific to that date. The photos taken at daylight showed about 150 Japanese fighter planes on the two fields. We were to go in with about twelve B-24s. The bombers were to be covered by about one hundred fighters: Marine, Army, Navy, and New Zealand. In the briefing, I literally begged the intelligence officer to have the 24s hit the field so that the Japanese fighter planes would not be able to take off. Targets for the dive-bombers and the torpedo planes were the ships. Since high-level bombers cannot hit a moving target, my request was entirely logical. But by this time the Army Air Force was running Strike Command, and the B-24 leader did not want to have the job of bombing the runways, so he led in on the ships. We all knew that some of us would not get back. Showalter came to me. He was to get on the transport to go home that morning before we could get back from the flight. He said, "Mr. Mac, I have changed my mind and I don't want to go to flight school. Can't you get my orders canceled?" After talking with him for a while, I asked why he really wanted not to go home. His answer was, "If you go to Kahili without me you won't get back." I told him to get on that plane, and get back home, and that I would see him in the States. Years later he was in the Reserve Squadron with me in Birmingham for a short time before he went back into the regular Marine Corps where he retired as a lieutenant colonel. The hop went as planned. The dispatch from Halsey to Admiral Mitscher afterward was:

FROM: COM THIRD FLEET
SECRET
YOUR 170305 XTO YOU MITSCHER AND ALL CONCERNED
X GOD BLESS EACH AND EVERY ONE OF YOU X HALSEY
REF: (170305) IN COMPLIANCE REQUEST YOUR RECENT LETTER TO ME DESIRE REPORT MITSCHER SENT SHIPPING STRIKE 198 PLANES BUIN AREA 0925 LOVE TODAY X PRELIMINARY REPORT X FIVE OR SIX SHIPS SUNK X ONE TANKER X ONE CHARLIE LOVE OR DOG LOVE X THREE OR FOUR DOGS X SHOT DOWN FORTY ONE ZEROS FIVE FLOATS X SEVEN OUR PLANES MISSING OF WHICH FIVE ARE FIGHTERS X COMPLETE DETAILS FROM MITSCHER WHEN CHECKED.

Bill Cohron, the squadron intelligence officer, who flew as the author's rear-seat gunner on the first attack by dive-bombers on Kahili Airfield on Bougainville.

(A "Charlie Love" is a light cruiser; a "Dog Love" is a large destroyer; a "Dog" is a destroyer.)

None of our squadron's planes was lost. The Navy lost one SBD and one of the TBFs was lost. Bill Cohron, our intelligence officer and an ex-rearseat gunner, rode with me. As soon as we pulled out of the dive, Bill called for me to turn to the right, and I started to turn when I saw a swarm of Japanese fighters in that direction. Obviously, I did not turn in that direction. He explained later that he wanted to have the opportunity to shoot one down. I had gone into this attack so that Hap Simpson, on my wing as usual, would be the first to rendezvous. On this flight as on the others, Caldwell did not make the rendezvous. We all thought that surely he had been shot down, but he made it back to the field by himself without seeing a Japanese plane.

Pot Roberts was one of our original replacement pilots.

After our first tour, we never had any Japanese ships as targets—the most desirable targets since you could see the results immediately. Pot was not one of the eighteen scheduled for the strike. He immediately began to pull strings to get in the flight, and after some effort managed to give one of the others a quart of whiskey to change places with him. He did get a hit on one of the ships and said it was worth the price.

★ 11 ★

Jug Herlihy's Tale and More War Stories

George Herlihy, Jug, was the most disarming of all of our pilots. He was small, quiet, the most unassuming person you could have known, and initially, none of us appreciated his ability. His quiet nature belied his skill. On the first tour he flew, without a complaint, more hours (110) than any of us. One day while he was waiting to fly, a softball hit him on his thumb. The blow caused a compound dislocation which had to be set and sewn up, but he never missed a flight. During the third tour of duty, an oil line was shot away over Villa and Jug had to make a water landing. He was seen getting out of the plane, into his raft, and making shore on a deserted island. All of us tried to keep any message from being sent to his mother and father in Tucson as we knew that he was all right. We wanted to spare them the worry such a message would naturally cause. But the message was sent. Jug's story of this flight made not only all of the news but subsequently a comic book. It is one of those squadron stories that is worth repeating.

Getting Shot Down in New Georgias Air Strike on Kolombangara

Just as we started the attack stray shots from a dog fight between Zeros and Corsairs cut a line to the oil cooler. I completed the dive-bombing run and pulled out to the south. The engine froze and I made water landing on sea side of Wana Wana. There was a mild sea, smooth landing, and Simmons, my gunner, got out the raft and we both had plenty of time to get in with our parachutes. Paddled about 100 yards to shore. The raft was overturned in surf and we waded in and headed for jungle. I was in the lead and heard a loud gunshot. Hitting the deck I was sure we were ambushed until I found out that Simmons accidentally discharged his .45 while loading a round in the chamber. After hiding in jungle for a few hours, we pushed our way, dragging the raft about 200–300 yards across the island to the lagoon side. We spent the night in jungle wrapped up in our parachutes. Next morning we paddled northwest along the beach away from Munda which we knew was in Japanese hands. About thirty minutes after starting, we heard a loud thrashing on shore and observed a ten-to-fifteen-foot crocodile get into the water. (I had never known that crocodiles occupied salt-water lagoons.) Since the beach was smoother than that previously passed, we hid the raft and proceeded on foot. Sometime later, after climbing over a log, I came face to face with a native. I don't know which of us was the more frightened. His pidgin English was as bad as mine, but I understood that the Japanese were not on the island and that he would take me to their village. At their village, I was introduced to their head-man who spoke and understood pidgin English much better. He was also a real con man. (I believe his name was Sam.) We had been told not to give anything to the natives since they were being paid by the coastwatchers. Sam wanted our parachutes but didn't want us to tell the coastwatcher. After some bantering back and forth, I made him understand that I could not, but that I wanted him to report our location to the coastwatcher and I would ask the coastwatcher for permission to leave the parachutes with him. We wrote our names and serial numbers on a piece of paper for him and he dispatched a runner to the coastwatcher who was in the mountains on Kolombangara. Sam showed us to a hut to stay in and requested that we stay out of sight so we would not be spotted by a Japanese patrol. There were no women or children in the village, they having been evacuated out of fear for the Japanese. We were fed taro, yams, fish, and chicken. We drank fresh coconut milk from the green coconuts exclusively. During the four or five days on Wana Wana, the invasion of the New Georgias was in process. One day from our grandstand seat we watched as eleven of a flight of twelve Japanese Bettys were shot down by AA fire from the invading fleet. One lone surviving Betty scooted past us at low altitude on its way back. We counted six to eight planes falling in flames at the same time. Three or four days after our arrival the coastwatcher sent me a letter stating that he had instructed the natives to return us to the fleet in the New Georgias. About an hour before dark they put each of us in an outrigger canoe and instructed us to keep down so the Japanese on Munda would not spot us. We had to pass a mile or so past Munda point. Just before dark, blond-headed Simmons stuck his head up to look around, and the Japanese opened fire with an artillery piece. Since we were at extreme range, their fire was very inaccurate. The natives really dug in to speed up and the Japanese gave up after three or four rounds. A short time later one of our PT boats spotted us and took us on board. The PT boats were starting their night patrol against any possible resupply of Japanese shipping. (I believe the skipper's name was Kelley.) The boats were equipped with recently developed radar for spotting any objectives at night. They also had a Negro aboard since they could purportedly see better at night. Around midnight the boat was tracking a bogey on the radar. It turned out to be a rain squall, and while following it we ran up on a submerged coral reef at very low speed. The home base

SBDs over the New Georgia group of islands. In the background is the island of Kolombangara where there was a Japanese field, Villa. Jug Herlihy landed in the waters at the upper right when he was shot down.

was notified of our predicament by radio. Since the hull was not damaged, it was decided to wait for high tide (tides are very low in the area) and try to float off. High tide coincided with dawn and we were still stuck when the Japanese, who were a short distance away on Munda, saw us and started shelling. It was an eerie feeling standing on the open deck of a wooden boat that was serving as a target. Another PT boat that was standing by was backing up to throw us a line to try to tow us off when it ran aground on the same reef. At about the same time, we were finally hit with a round after what seemed like a dozen near-misses (probably four or five). Only one crew member was injured. A comical event (in retrospect) occurred when the Negro lookout on board announced to the skipper that he would signal the other boats that we had a man wounded. He stood up on the fantail, started some semaphore and fell overboard. The wounded man was put in a rubber life raft and everyone else from both boats jumped overboard and swam out to the other PTs for a fast getaway. Upon arrival at the base of the invading force, Simmons and I went aboard an LST for return to Guadalcanal that night. [The area where Jug landed was the same area future President Kennedy's PT boat was cut in half and the PTs who rescued him were from his squadron.]

The overnight trip to Guadalcanal was uneventful except for being awakened several times by loud explosions that sounded as though we had been torpedoed. It was just the flat bottom of the LST slamming down in the rough seas. The next morning we walked into camp and continued normal operations.

Prior to that time Jug had asked that his tour of duty be extended so he could have one tour of duty in fighters, but after returning to base he changed his mind. He later did a tour of duty in fighters and during the Korean War was an outstanding night-fighter pilot.

Jack Sperzel was the fastidious one of us. He had been reared as the only child of a wealthy family, and it took some time for many of us to appreciate him. Before Captain Spang arrived, Jack recognized that someone had to handle the squadron operations, and he undertook that job. He had been in the squadron since it was reorganized while at NAS San Diego and looked upon himself as a plank owner. On our first tour, because he was acting as operations officer, he flew only about half as much as the rest of us, and for some reason I never flew with him. While I said nothing, I resented being sent out on the searches and attacks while he stayed back. I was dead wrong. Captain Spang, the squadron operations officer, did not get to the Canal until November 17 and he was killed on his second flight. Sperz undertook the job because he recognized that it had to be done. When we returned to Espiritu Santo for rest camp and reorganization, I was disgusted that Sperzel and I were assigned to the same tent. It was the best thing that could have happened to me. I was given the opportunity to get to know one of the finest men I have ever met. He was completely unselfish and always ready to carry more than his share of the load.

Fifteen of us left Cactus still in flight status on December 24. Six had been killed, two were sent out because they were not able to take the mental strain, two for adverse reaction to malaria and for other health-related causes, and Paul Kellogg had crashed and was severely burned. During the month of January, we lost both Walt Eck and Bill Hronek in operational accidents, and E. P. McBryde was sent home for medical reasons. During the latter part of January and first part of February 1943, we were given thirteen pilots as replacements. Six had no combat experience, and the other seven had done a short tour of duty at Guadalcanal with VMSB-142 after we were relieved. We were particularly fortunate in the caliber and the attitude of these replacements. They were all first-class pilots and fitted in with our squadron in its flying and in its play. As could be expected, some of them proved to be real characters as we grew to know them. The biggest one of all was Frank Pope. Frankie was from Nanticoke, Pennsylvania, a big hulk of a man, thoroughly disarming. He appeared slow of wit and of movement, but it was merely a facade to cover up a smart and kindly person. Frankie was a Phi Beta Kappa and had been a contestant in the heavyweight division of the Golden Gloves just before the war. He was assigned to my division and flew wing on me for a time. An excellent pilot, he had several habits that were hard to break. Most of our flights were of about four hours duration, and we wore helmets that were not designed for comfort. In order to hear, they had to fit tightly over the ears, so that after a flight of that length our ears would be hurting. Frankie habitually took off his helmet on the way home from an attack and hung it on the gunsight, the telescope that was right in front of your face. If the flight leader had any information that needed to be passed out to the flight, or if some message came in for us or from anyone else, I had to signal Frankie to get his helmet on so that he could hear. I explained the problem to him several times, but in his good-natured way he always said something to the effect that I worried too much and not to worry about him. Frankie was one of the replacements who had never been to Guadalcanal and had never seen a Zero. There was very naturally a great deal of curiosity about these planes and the Japanese tactics. I made it up with the remaining pilots of our division and all of the gunners to teach Frankie a lesson that he would remember.

We planned to simulate an attack by Japanese fighters when we were returning from a mission and knew we were safe. The rear-seat gunners were to shoot on signal. On the appointed day when we were on the way home, Frankie, as was his custom, took off his helmet and hung it on the gunsight. We flew for a period of time, and then I picked up the radio and called for the simulated attack. Frankie grabbed for his helmet, and I immediately made an abrupt turn toward him. For a wingman to fly close formation required both hands and intense concentration on the flight leader's plane. Frankie could not get his helmet. All twelve of the rear-seat guns of the entire formation were firing. We straightened out. Frankie again reached for his helmet. We turned sharply away from him and again he could not reach the helmet. We continued these tactics until all of the ammunition in the rear-seat guns was expended. Meanwhile, Frankie had dropped his helmet on the floor of the plane. He finally retrieved it and called to find out what had happened. When no one replied, Frankie thought his transmitter was not working. As soon as we landed, he rushed to me and asked what had happened. We had to watch him for the rest of the tour because it was obvious that he would try to get even with us. But he flew with his helmet on for the remainder of the time.

All of the replacements had newer clothes, shoes, and

watches than the rest of us. Most of ours had worn out, ceased to operate, or been lost. Frankie roomed with Hap, Chuck, and me when we returned to Cactus. He had a fine new watch and some good fighter boots which were his pride. Whenever we were put up for an attack the next day, we told some tall tale about where we were going and all of the hazards of the flight. One of us would say to Frankie, "Don't wear your good watch tomorrow. We probably are going to lose you and there's no sense in losing that watch. Hap needs a new watch." Or one of us pretended to want his fighter boots. Frankie's answer was that we ought not to talk like that because if he was shot down, we'd be sorry. Or that we sounded like ghouls dividing his effects before he was gone. He had a good sense of humor; otherwise, we would have driven him crazy.

We went to Sydney for another week's rest and recreation after our second tour. At the end of the week we left the hotel, going to the airport seated at the rear end of a flatbed truck. When the truck stopped for a red light, Frankie jumped off and picked up a small kitten, obviously lost, and brought it back to Espiritu where he raised it. It was his constant companion. Whenever we flew anywhere for overnight away from the island for any purpose, Frankie would put the cat "Damit" in a mosquito net, one designed to cover a steel helmet, and hang it on the gunsight. Damit went everywhere, including our last tour at Guadalcanal. Damit grew to be a young cat. None of us ever saw another cat anywhere out there, but about the time the original pilots in the squadron were to be relieved and sent home, it was obvious that Damit had located a tomcat, for she was in a family way. We never were able to ascertain the father or where he came from. Since Frankie was a replacement, he was required to complete one more tour of duty at Cactus prior to being sent home, and about two to three months later we knew Frankie had returned because Damit and her story were on the front page of the San Diego paper. Frankie had brought Damit home with him. The paper carried a big picture of Damit on page one.

Frankie was sent home on leave with orders to return to

Jack Sperzel and John Stock with natives of Guadalcanal. The natives worked with the coastwatchers in rescuing pilots when lost or shot down in the Solomon Islands.

the west coast for duty. He took Damit to a vet in San Diego to board during his leave, and, as was the case in many instances, during his leave his orders were changed to east coast duty. The vet bills mounted, and the vet threatened to do away with Damit. Frankie told him what a notorious and valuable cat she was and told him to keep her, that he would pick her up at some later time. Almost a year later Frankie was sent overseas again and went by the vet, paid Damit's bill, and took her overseas with him again.

Another of our replacements was John Stock. John was from Storm Lake, Iowa, and had taught school and coached football prior to going to flight school. He and Sperzel had been in the same flight class and he had been in 132 prior to its being sent overseas. After the Battle of Midway, he and Jack McGuckin, another of the replacements, had been sent to Midway for training and to conduct antisub patrols. They had both been replacement pilots for 142 after we were relieved at Cactus. John, Sperzel, and I were all in the same flight class, though John and Sperz graduated at Corpus Christi and I finished at Pensacola. John was an extremely capable individual and a natural leader. When we returned to the States, he and I were the CO and executive officer of 141 when it was reformed. After Major Robertshaw was ordered to group as operations officer, the squadron was divided into two attack groups, John leading one and I the other. On one occasion after we arrived at Guadalcanal on our third and last tour, Stock led a nine-plane strike on a Japanese airfield at Villa near Munda. His story of the mission follows.

June 30, 1943. It was what the Aussie Coast Watchers called a "snake front." This type of pea soup weather started at sea level, went up over twenty thousand feet, and extended in a long, narrow, high, nebulous mass, oscillating back and forth like a serpent. Here it was, the third day of this lousy weather front and the brass said our attacking ground forces for the New Georgia campaign needed some air power to knock out the Japanese air strip located at Villa Point on Kolombangara Island, just across Kula Gulf from our main ground offensive near Munda. The Japs were sending down every airplane they could get into the air from Kahili and harassing our assault troops, supply barges, shipping, and so on. After dropping their loads and strafing, they would land at Villa, refuel, rebomb and rearm, then quickly attack again. They were able to do this because of the bad weather that stretched between Henderson Field on Guadalcanal and the New Georgia Islands. Sometimes a few of our fighters from the strip on the Russell Islands were getting over the top on oxygen and also there was a Marine fighter squadron flying Corsairs from a new small strip that the Seabees had just built on some recently captured real estate at the southeast tip of the New Georgia Islands. These Marine fighters were doing great, considering the storm and the distance they had to go for refueling and rearming.

It was VMSB-132's turn to try and get through the

lousy storm that was "gumming up the works." Nine dive-bombers, plus six torpedo bombers from VMTB-131, took off and headed up the slot. There it was, ahead of us, that menacing mass of thunderheads, fog, rain, and gray goop. We couldn't go under it, others had tried, or over it because it was too high for our heavy bomb and fuel load. Also, our oxygen equipment was not as trustworthy as we would have liked. We started climbing to attain "bomb run" altitude with hopes of finding a way through or around this so-called tropical disturbance. The turbulence could bounce fifteen airplanes around like toy boats in a washing machine. We turned left, then right, then left again in order to gain the altitude we needed before attempting to go through the storm. On our last turn I spotted a hole in the mass at about 13,000 feet and we headed for it. It was like going through a tunnel and, sure enough, there was light at the other end of it. I thought we had really lucked out! There was Villa Air Strip ahead of us, maybe five minutes or less from a diving position. I looked around. There were a lot of big, billowy white clouds, and off to the left, about five miles away, I spotted at least ten or twelve fighter planes going at it in a big dog fight. I recognized the gull wings of a Corsair on one of the planes; I felt a little better knowing that we had some of our own fighters to help us. One Zero was on us almost immediately, guns blinking red, with a Corsair on his tail. Lieutenant McGuckin, my right wingman, got peppered good but hung in there. Another Jap was coming up from below. Lieutenant Herlihy, leader of the third section, was also hit and fell out of formation. Both of his wingmen followed him down. Thank goodness, for those few Corsairs most certainly prevented a lot more of us from being knocked out.

The rest of us continued on to Villa with the TBFs breaking off to make their run from a lower elevation.

They would go in and glide bomb after we made our dive. I was pushing over into my dive when "Hot Damn," I spotted a Zero making a landing approach to Villa Air Strip. I broke radio silence (which was okay now that we had reached the target), and told the others of my find. I was in my dive and couldn't bring my guns to bear because he was just coming onto the runway and I was heading for a spot right in the middle. I strafed going down, then released the one-thousand-pound bomb, hoping that the Jap plane would run into the explosion as he was completing his landing, or that the very large hole the bomb would create in the runway would grab him in some way as he went by, or, maybe, he would die of a heart attack or something! No such wishful thinking on McGuckin's part. As he went into his dive, only seconds after I did, he saw the Zero, released his bomb from a higher elevation than we generally do (he still got a good hit), and found the Jap, fat, dumb, and happy, right in his sights. He opened up with his front guns, twin fifty-calibers, and the Zero made one-half of a slow roll and landed upside down, skidding off the runway. This was a large and unusual feat, a slow, overloaded, underpowered dive-bomber shooting down a sleek, fast fighter, regardless of circumstances. It was like a barnyard chicken knocking a golden eagle out of the sky.

When I was pulling out of my dive and clearing out of the Villa Point area, like a scared rabbit (as we all usually do), my plane took a hell of a jolt. We had taken a hit from some smaller caliber automatic ground weapon, probably a twenty millimeter. Sergeant Miller, my radio gunner, said he was okay and the plane flew great. I saw no fuel or oil leaks and the gauges were normal. Luck was still with us! I started to fly a big easy circle so the scattered planes could join up. At this altitude the weather conditions were again bad—low-hanging clouds, pelting rain, and poor visibility. The torpedo planes joined in the formation and we headed back. We were missing Herlihy, his two wingmen, and two other planes from the first division.

The weather got worse. We were now flying very low, just above the white caps, and under the front we had avoided rather easily on the way up. It was like the inside of a whale's belly. We couldn't see a thing except the water. The torpedo planes pulled away and went ahead. We were too slow for them. Their planes had more power and were much faster than ours. They also had radar and in this kind of weather would home right into Henderson Field with no problem. They had done a good job, and so had we. We had plastered the runway of Villa Air Strip. Of course, it was an easy target and a miss would have been unusual. Both outfits knew how to bomb.

We now had been cruising along on our return leg for about an hour. The weather was getting better, visibility a mile or two, maybe three at times. I had an uncomfortable feeling. Something was wrong. Fuel was low, but I had enough. The hit by AA at Villa had still not given us any problem. My heading was okay, or was it? We generally came back along the slot but not this time. I had made proper compensation for the change. The wind had been very strong at times, but I had made allowances for this, too. I had become spoiled, accustomed to seeing reference points on a clear day such as Santa Isabel, Wickham Anchorage, Russell Islands, and Savo. Well, Cape Esperance should show up any time now. I called Miller on the intercom. "Turn on the loop and see if you can pick up a heading to Henderson Field."

The loop was an old radio homing aid which had been used in aviation for a number of years. Guadalcanal had installed a station a while back but, at low altitudes, when the mountains were between you and the station sending the signal, poor reception was the general rule.

The sound signal we got was very weak. Must be the mountains. Also, the static was bad due to the poor weather. Miller swung the loop back and forth. No clear indicator here! About this time the rear three planes in our formation turned left away from our group. They were probably short on fuel and decided to go into the Russells for gas. They probably had called on the radio to tell us but we weren't receiving. Miller had turned everything off except the loop and the intercom to reduce static and improve reception. I checked my gauges and still felt I had enough fuel to get us home. In formation flying, the farther back in the squadron, the more gas your plane will use, due to more and greater throttle changes to keep in position, and in turns, you cover more distance than the guys near the front. I had to consider the fuel situation in the other planes. It could be coming to a critical stage. I called Miller again. "Put the loop in a straight forward position. I'll climb higher and make an easy right turn in hopes of getting a better signal and we will try to get a build or a fade."

We tried it and I listened carefully, but could not make a determination. The weather was getting better but reception did not improve and, of course, I knew by now that we had missed Guadalcanal. Probably the turn did it. Lost. I'll be damned! I was getting a fade now in the loop radio signal. We were going away from the radio station at Henderson. Well, we will make a 180-degree turn and head for home but as I started to turn, I saw in the distance, to the south, a tiny island and beyond that another larger island. Better take a quick look. These must be Bellona and Rennell islands. Couldn't be anything else. I called Miller again. "Go back on regular frequency and see if you can get through to Henderson Field."

McGuckin waggled his wings. I looked over and he was talking into his mike. I received only static and garbled words. The hits he took from the first Zero had partially damaged his radio. He could hear us fairly well but couldn't send, so through elaborate sign language on his part he let me know that he was low on fuel and that we should check out the island a little further. My gauges showed that a return to Guadalcanal was maybe possible but it would be risky, especially if we had to fly around bad weather. However, if I was low on gas the others were in even more dire straits than I. What to do?

Rennell was a long island, about forty miles long and approximately ten miles wide. It had a land-locked lake at the east end, obviously the crater of an extinct volcano. The land around the lake was elevated in most places, to the extent that the surface of the water had protection from the wind. I looked at the ocean where large swells and spraying white caps were quite evident. I talked to Otteson and Bachtel, the other two pilots from our squadron. There was also a fighter pilot in a Corsair that had been following us. He was on a different frequency than we were, and he couldn't be raised on the radio. My conclusion was to ditch in the lake. If we were going to put the planes down in the water some place, it would be best to do so near an island and not in the middle of nowhere, where the chances of being found were nil. Best to land where the top of the water was not such a maelstrom as the surface of the ocean was right now. I informed the others.

I had spotted a native village at the west end of the lake. No evidence of Japs anywhere. I told Miller to prepare for a water landing. We had a procedure in Marine dive-bomber squadrons for ditching the plane in water. It was updated from time to time, and the pilots and radio gunners reviewed the program during training periods when we were not in combat. The process for survival went something like this:

"The radio-gunner jettisons the canopy which

covered his cockpit and secures the twin machine guns so they do not swing around at impact and break his arm or head. He gathers anything in the second seat which could be of value to the crew for rescue or survival purposes such as Very pistols, shells, first-aid kit, maps, charts, and so forth. He then unhooks his safety belt, slips out of his parachute harness, rehooks his safety belt, checks his life jacket; removes his goggles, faces forward with arms braced against the forward part of his cockpit, protects his face and head with his forearms, flight jacket, or any other padding available in case of a hard landing. After the plane has come to a stop on the water, he quickly releases his safety belt, jumps out of the cockpit onto the left wing, opens the hatch at the side of the plane which houses the two-man rubber boat and pulls it out. He lays the life raft on the wing and inflates it by pulling a loop cord attached to a CO^2 cylinder. Upon inflation, he places the raft in the water, aft of the wing, holds it close with the attached bow rope so the pilot, after getting out of his cockpit onto the wing, can step into the boat. The gunner shoves off and jumps into the raft. Both pilot and gunner break out an oar and paddle away from the sinking plane.

The pilot in the meantime, while the gunner is doing all these chores, goes through a 'May Day' procedure, giving their location by voice radio, then jettisons his cockpit enclosure, gathers any items from the front seat which may be of value later, takes off his goggles, and disconnects radio and oxygen connections. Upon coming to a stop, after landing, he releases his safety belt, unbuckles his shoulder straps, and tugs himself out of his parachute. He then turns on the switch which destroys the IFF equipment and any other secret gear that may be wired to an explosive charge. (This destruction of secret equipment had a built-in delay which allowed the crew to get clear of the plane before it exploded.) The pilot then steps out on the wing with his gathered paraphernalia and steps into the life raft which is waiting."

That's the way it's supposed to go but in this case, it didn't go like that at all. After the plane had stopped on the water, I finally struggled out of the cockpit, onto the wing, ready to step into the rubber boat; but it was stuck, inflated halfway in and halfway out of the hatch opening of the compartment where it had been stored. Miller wasn't anywhere in sight but a few seconds later he came struggling to the surface of the water—nearly drowned. While pulling the raft out of the storage compartment, he had accidentally inflated it and it had stuck in the plane. Miller had then pulled the cords that inflated his "Mae West," and jumped into the water to get closer to the raft in the hope of freeing it from its grasping tomb. His life jacket did not inflate! Before landing he had put two Very pistols, about thirty flare-shells, a first-aid kit, camera and other items from his compartment inside his flight suit. These items were held in place around the middle by his belt and were kept from falling out by the zipper. He also had all his personal survival gear, such as a 45-caliber pistol, ammunition, food packet, another first-aid kit, hunting knife, canteen, and the like. The whole lot probably weighed over thirty pounds. When he hit the water, he sank like a rock. What I mean, deep!

I inflated my Mae West, jumped in, grabbed him by the shoulder of his flight suit, and held his head out of water while I worked him over to the wing of the plane. He dumped the stuff from the inside of his flight suit, then came over to help me try and get the life raft out of the plane. We failed. We had to get out of there. The plane was sinking. The explosive charge could go off any time. We had also been told that it would not be real smart to be close to the plane when it sank because it was possible to be pulled underwater by the vortex, a suction that is created when the aircraft sinks.

We swam away. Our progress would not have reminded you of Johnny Weissmuller, but we were able to get approximately thirty feet from the aircraft before it sank.

After about fifteen or twenty seconds, a small miracle occurred. The life raft came shooting out of the water, high into the air, and settled back down, floating on the surface fully inflated. Either the pressure of the deep water or the IFF destruct charge had kicked it out and sent it right back to us.

In the interim, McGuckin and Otteson had landed their planes in the water about 100 and 200 yards from us. Bachtel landed quite a bit further down the lake and the fighter pilot circled around a while and then landed even farther east.

Our raft was upside down. We tried to right it but the wind was giving us a lot of trouble. I could see several outrigger canoes that had put out from shore coming toward us. As they got closer, you could see that all the people, in each canoe, were young girls between the ages of maybe thirteen and twenty-five. They had very light-colored skin, Polynesian-type. Some even had copper-colored hair. Shades of Fletcher Christian, they were really beautiful and bare to the waist.

To hell with the raft! Those canoes looked great to me and very welcome. I told Miller, whose life vest was still not inflated, to crawl aboard one of the canoes. He tried. The girls squealed, screamed, giggled, and backed away. They let us know in a hurry that the canoe would tip over; it was full, booked up. They spoke only one word of English, slang English that is, and the word was "okay." Generally, they combined it into a four-syllable word and nearly always answered in this way, "Okay-Okay." They were having a great time, yelling, squealing, and giggling. Miller and I finally got the raft right-side up, and climbed aboard. McGuckin, with his gunner, Sergeant Kretz, and Otteson, with his gunner, Sergeant Chapin, were paddling toward us in their rubber rafts. They looked like drowned rats, but were in good shape and had their share of native girls in canoes following them.

We paddled ashore, being led by some of the canoes, and pulled into a small, protected bay which was surrounded on the shore side with native huts which made up the village I had seen from the air. The men and older boys had evidently been on a food safari when we landed in the water and were now just returning. We were welcomed by the chief. His name was Kasipa and he could speak a limited amount of pidgin English. All the natives were fair-skinned, many with light reddish-brown hair, bleached even lighter by the sun and the water. They were average or medium in size, friendly, and courteous. Both the women and men dressed in a short-skirted loin cloth combination made of cotton cloth. Some of the cloth had printed patterns decorating the otherwise drab material.

Most of us were wet and the wind seemed a little cold. We built a fire to dry our clothes and survival gear. The entire village population were spectators to our "strip tease" act. We peeled down to our shorts and hung our clothes and gear on sticks near the fire. I had a package of cigarettes that I thought I had waterproofed in a rubber wrapper, but it had leaked and they had gotten a bit wet. I very carefully took each cigarette from the package and placed them, one by one, on a rock next to the fire. I noticed intense interest by the small fry in my work, and the moment I laid down the last cigarette, they all rushed in, both boys and girls, and they each grabbed one of the damp tailor-mades and lit up with a brand from the fire. They didn't seem to care if they were wet or not. Obviously from this action, in addition to the one-word vocabulary of

Okay-Okay, the pidgin English spoken by the chief, and the printed cloth used for clothing, these people had had some connection with folks other than themselves and the Japanese in the recent past.

It was getting late. Our clothes were dry. We put them on, ate some of our survival rations, plus some native food, and then lay down near the fire. The chief offered us an empty hut which we turned down. We took turns standing guard during the night.

The next morning, the chief, after much gesticulating and pidgin English, led us to understand that he was going to send us to the main village at the other end of the lake. There we would have a better chance of being rescued. We made ready to go. Our toilet habits were handicapped. The lack of soap, razors, toothbrushes, and combs was not so bad, but when the urge to relieve ourselves came, we were followed wherever we went by fifteen or twenty children (both sexes), a few young adults (both sexes), and two or three older women. We solved the problem to some degree by walking rapidly up a path into the jungle and then jumping quickly behind a tree before anyone could catch up. We also went swimming a lot.

We shoved off, leaving our life rafts, our new friends, and the chief behind. Kasipa had given me a beautiful hand-carved war stick of dark hardwood (could have been ebony) with mother of pearl designs embedded in the handle. I thanked him and gave him my pocket compass in return.

They had fixed up the outrigger canoes so that a bamboo platform about six feet square ran between the main hull and the outrigger attachment. There were three such canoes and we were to ride, like royalty, two Marines on each platform. There would be two natives paddling each rig. It was a beautiful day. The wind had died down and the lake had just a ripple. There were wild ducks flying all over the place. We had gotten started by 0600. We followed the shoreline along the south side of the lake. The natives, sturdy in build, kneeling on the bottom of the canoe, kept a steady pace and metronome timing in their paddling strokes. It looked as if they could paddle all day long. To our amazement, this is exactly what happened. We did not realize that the main village was so far. It took over ten hours to get there.

During the day, all of us tried our hands at paddling but it was hard work, we tired quickly, and our hands blistered. Around noon we pulled into a bay that was surrounded on the short side by a rather large, near level valley with beautiful tropical foliage and hundreds of coconut trees. I had been worried about food. The natives had not brought any with them. We had broken out the limited supply of "C" rations and flight rations that we carry in waterproof containers in a pouch attached to a regular issue web belt that we wear around our waists. Also attached is our 45-caliber automatic handgun, ammunition, hunting knives, first-aid kit, and other assorted kits and items that each individual thinks he might need in case he is forced down. We shared some of the rations with our volunteer galley friends. They liked it very much and asked for more. We gave them more, though I felt we should conserve, but what are you going to do? We also had to keep steam in our locomotive.

Upon coming ashore, some of the native men disappeared; others started climbing coconut trees. They scooted up the trees like monkeys and cut down several green coconuts with their long machetes. Minutes later, with the same knives, they sliced off a number of thin, round pieces of husk from the nut about the size of a jelly jar lid. Next they cut off the top quarter of the coconut, drank the juice and then scooped out the white inside of the nut with the sliver that was sliced from the outer surface of the coconut and ate the contents with relish. This was really a demonstration for our benefit. One of them gave each of us a "husk spoon" and chopped the top off of a number of green coconuts. We drank the juice. Great! We ate the creamy nut interior which was about the consistency of custard pudding and tasted just like coconut cream pie. Delicious!

The other guides had returned during our lesson in eating coconuts. They had bananas and other fruits and vegetables that I did not recognize. One vegetable must have been breadfruit which had been baked and stored in this way-station. It was about twice the size of a large potato, with a white, starchy pulp interior and mealy in consistency. We ate this with our home-made spoons. Not bad. Not bad at all.

We didn't linger long. No demitasse or Napoleon brandy. The escorts wanted to get going. They knew we still had a long way to go. Late in the afternoon they pointed out the village in the distance. We arrived about 1700 and were greeted by all the folks in the community. Again when we spoke to almost any of the people, we got the same answer, "Okay-Okay."

The chief's name was Teketa, evidently the number one guy of the whole island. He had a larger vocabulary and spoke better pidgin English than Kasipa. We asked him to thank our guides. They were tired, but far from exhausted, and peppy enough to dart here and there to greet their many friends and relatives in the village. As for the six U.S. Marines (cream of the American youth), we were depleted.

On our voyage from the first village, we had looked carefully for Bachtel and Salmon, his gunner, and also the fighter pilot, but did not see any sign of them. We had hoped they would be here in this village, but again we were disappointed. I was sure they were all right—just a gut feeling that this was true.

The people here looked and dressed the same as the good people of the first village. There was but one flaw in their otherwise handsome outward appearance. Nearly all the men over the age of thirty and many of the older women had black teeth. Their lips were very red and their gums looked inflamed, as if infected. Some had teeth that appeared decayed or rotten. Their problem was from chewing the betel nut, common among natives in the South Pacific. Evidently, the younger people did not eat the stuff or it took a while for the bad appearances to take effect. I found it interesting to see how greatly the natives of the different islands varied in physical appearance. For example, the natives on Espiritu Santo were small, slight in build, brown-skinned, many with straight hair and all with definite oriental eyes and facial features. The natives of Guadalcanal, less than 100 miles from Rennell, were large, well-built, husky, very dark people with curly hair, any one of the men looking like he could step in and easily play middle linebacker for the Green Bay Packers. Then there were the light-skinned, copper-haired, medium-sized people of Rennell whom I have already described. Unusual homesteading, to say the least!

We were given a large hut for our use. It was constructed from local trees, bamboo, and palm fronds. The floor was about four feet off the ground, made of woven fiber materials, and had one-inch square holes left in the matting in a checkerboard pattern. At night, this natural air conditioning made sleeping cool. In the daytime the circulation caused the interior to be tolerable.

I talked to the chief about the possibility of being rescued. He assured me that a plane which landed and took off on water would come along. "When?" I asked, and was informed that it would be in one or two moons.

One of the first things Teketa wanted to know was, who was the chief of our group. Otteson and McGuckin pointed to me. We were all of the same rank but I was a little bit senior, so got the nod as "Big Cheese" of our little detachment. After this, he talked mostly to me. He was quite intent in telling me about some trouble he was having and his wife was part of it. I tried to get him off the subject for I didn't want to get involved in a family argument, but he was quite insistent. Many people could have understood him quite well, but I just didn't have an ear for pidgin English or any other foreign language for that matter. I flunked French my first semester in college, which indicates my capabilities along these lines. "I am very sorry, but I do not understand all that you are trying to tell me, Teketa, and I am very tired and want to sleep, so let's talk about this problem tomorrow."

We had eaten our evening meal. Part of the food had come from our rations which were nearly gone, and some of it was native food. I called the flyers together for a meeting in our hut. We discussed our problems and what to do about them. McGuckin was assigned the task of getting food. He queried, "Where will I get all this food you are talking about? I haven't seen any neighborhood grocery store around here."

I had been an ardent bird hunter before joining the Marines and the abundance of wild ducks around the lake fascinated me. "Well, you can start by getting some ducks," I said. "There are hundreds of wild ducks around here." McGuckin asked, "With what, a sharp stick?"

"No," I told him. "All you have to do is shoot them with that .45 you have hanging from your belt. I've noticed you can get real close to them. Besides, it shouldn't be difficult for a sharpshooter like you. After all, anyone who can shoot down a Jap Zero should be able to fill the larder with duck. You can also talk to the native women with your special sign language, and also the chief. I am sure they will have many suggestions as to how to get some food."

Otteson and his gunner, Sergeant Chapin, were put in charge of getting all of our gear back in shape again: Very pistols, shells, knives, first-aid kits, rations, compasses, flashlights, and so on. These items needed drying out, cleaning, rust removed, and proper storage. The other two gunners were put in charge of rescue signals. They helped with the flare-guns and panels, gathered firewood, and the like. I took the job of trying to find out what happened to Bachtel, his radio-gunner, and the fighter pilot.

The next day the chief came up with an unopened gallon tin of chili con carne and another gallon tin of diced carrots. It seems that headquarters at Guadalcanal had put a small detachment of Marines on Rennell Island in the early stages of the Solomon campaign. They were there about a month or so, patrolled the island, and kept a lookout for Japanese attempts to take over. They also sent radio reports on weather and plane sightings. The Japanese had also been on the island earlier. The chief showed me a couple of wrecked Jap landing craft on the beach. Anyway, thanks to former Marine occupation of the island, we now added carrots and chili to our hoarded supply of food.

Teketa was anxious for me to go see his wife, who I had gathered by now was sick or incapacitated in some way. Off we went, deep into the jungle, following a rather newly cleared path. We walked at least one-half mile and came to an open area with several newly built, temporary, "lean-to" type enclosures. We went to the largest of these. Here were three older native women and a very young girl. She looked about fourteen years old, obviously very pregnant and in pain. This was the chief's wife, which surprised me somewhat because he looked to be about forty-five to fifty years old. He wanted me to help her. I checked her pulse rate and it was normal. I felt her forehead, and she seemed to have a fever. I took four sulpha-thyazol tablets from my first-aid kit and had her swallow one with water. I gave the remainder to the head midwife and got her to understand that the girl should take one each day. I didn't feel that one pill a day would hurt her and they might even do her some good. We left. The chief seemed pleased. Evidently my bedside manner had made a fair impression and he thanked me several times. I tried to impress on him, however, that I was not a doctor, and I was not able to help much.

Again he started to talk to me quite rapidly, with great excitement in his voice, but I was unable to piece together his ideas. He realized this and held up one finger, as if he had just thought of a great idea. His eyes shone with eagerness. "Wait one, quick time. Teketa come back me."

Well, I wasn't figuring on catching a bus at that time anyway, so I waited. I wanted to try to get more information from the chief on a possible search by some of his people for our missing airmen. After a bit, I wandered over to where the gunners were working on the flare-guns, flare-shells, signal fire, and other "help wanted" devices. About three hours after he had left me, Teketa reappeared with a sheet of paper, torn from a bound, ledger-type account book. He had written a letter to me, hoping that this would help me understand his problem and that I would react favorably. The letter went like this:

Chief:

Please Sir my friends big Master at in here my place call his name Tingoa and call this land Rennel Island. Nice Chief help me please now I will squeal you one troubled I have now here. My wife have Picnnin in stomach ache hurt everytime. Chief please you must sendim your help full come. We here in Rennell you must let doctor come please him healing nice all manner of sickness. I keep wife in my house every time but me no savey. Watch give medicine along wife because me no have something for heal this sick that is the way me ask you.

Chief please help me for healing my wife please all time have sickness not eat no drink me sad too much my wife very sick this time about Doctor him come with you in here now? Suppose the Doctor come he very nice to me here you must help me for healing this sick suppose you no have medicine for heal my wife about next boat or plane come stay here him savey take me and wife sick go with you in plane go in quiet place of doctor for help good.

I know you fella americans very nice.

I are your friend

I am is my name

Teketa

I still have the original letter among my souvenirs and mementos of World War II.

I assured Teketa that I would do the best I could. I was sure that once a plane came something would be done and not to worry.

Of course, I was curious as to how he had learned to write. He showed me inside their largest hut. At one end was a raised platform with a handmade pulpit and chair standing on it. The rest of the area was filled with rustic wood benches. An aisle was open down the center. This was the village church. Here they prayed and sang hymns. Missionaries had helped them build the chapel and had taught the chiefs to read and write. The sons of the different chiefs were sent to schools on the big island, wherever that was. When the war came, the missionaries were forced to leave. They were missed.

The day passed. McGuckin had done well with the food problem, but no ducks. The others of our group had completed their work and in good fashion, too. Only I, the so-called chief, had not accomplished much. Teketa tried to assure me that our missing companions were all right and indicated that we could start taking a look around tomorrow.

We went to church that night. We listened to the village people sing hymns. The tunes were familiar—"Onward Christian Soldiers," "Jesus Loves Me," and others, but the words were quite garbled.

The next day around 1000 we heard the sound of an aircraft. The natives were quite excited—we were delirious. We stayed out of sight until we identified the plane. It was a PBY flying boat, the ugliest airplane in the Navy, but to us it was as beautiful as Hedy LaMarr. We started a fire, put green branches on it so it would smoke good, shot off flares, and ran around like crazy chickens.

The PBY took its time, followed the shore line of the lake on the south side and then came back along the north side. It then went around again, making a smaller circle, landed on the water and taxied into the bay in front of the village. Several Navy officers and enlisted men got out and came ashore. They seemed more interested in talking to the natives than to us. I guess this was understandable, especially when it was beautiful, young, bare-breasted girls they were trying to converse with. These girls were again giggling and laughing and showing off their English—"Okay-Okay."

I did learn that one of us had gotten through on the radio to Henderson Field before ditching and they had picked up the location of our forced landing. A rescue plane had not come before because there was still some bad weather around the Canal, and they wanted it as clear as possible for any search that might need to be made. They had also seen signs of our other airmen down the lake a few miles and planned to pick them up as soon as they left here. This was indeed good news, but the bad news was that there was not a doctor on board and no one could help Teketa's wife. The "P" boat captain couldn't take the responsibility of having an overdue, pregnant woman on board without proper attendance of a doctor or nurse. He was quite sure that such personnel could be brought back when they made the "beef run." It seems that we were not the first to be marooned on this island. For each flyer the natives rescued they were rewarded with a case of canned beef, a sack of flour, and a sack of beans. These and other supplies would be brought back, probably the next day.

I found Teketa talking earnestly to the PBY pilot and co-pilot. We all explained to him that the doctor would come. Just before climbing aboard, the chief gave me another native carved war stick. The ebony weapons must have a symbolic meaning of some kind, for their actual value as a fighting aid had obviously deteriorated over the last several generations. I gave him my hunting knife and signaling mirror, thanking him again for all he had done for us.

We took off, then landed again farther down the lake and picked up our buddies. There was a lot of back slapping and hand shaking. They were in good shape and had a lot of tales of their own to tell.

Returning to Henderson Field was almost as good as returning home. We briefed all the brass and departments who were concerned with our entire episode. I got assurances from the officer of the day that medical help would be sent to Rennell Island to aid the chief's wife and make routine health checks on any of the others who wanted help. Later I heard that volunteers were asked for among medical people on Guadalcanal. The PBY was to return the next day. Nearly every doctor on the base was bidding for a chance to go.

We were taken to our bivouac area and the first person we saw was Captain McEniry, the squadron's flight leader. When he saw us he could hardly believe his eyes. They had not heard anything from the wing as to our whereabouts or rescue. Others came out of the follies (quonset huts) and again there was much back slapping, hand shaking, yelling, and snide remarks about some people taking weekend vacations.

I found out that all the others on that particular flight to Villa Point had made out all right. Herlihy and Simmons returned safely a couple of days after we did, which completed the group.

I also heard that Teketa's wife had her baby and both were doing well, so you might say that everything turned out "Okay-Okay."

The natives on Guadalcanal were just like the blacks in the South in appearance. All except those on Bougainville and Malaita were friendly. The natives on Bougainville were closely watched—and controlled—by the Japanese. We were told that there were two types of natives on Malaita, those who lived in houses built over the water on the coast who were friendly and those in the mountains who were cannibals. No one, to my knowledge, ever went down on Malaita. We were briefed not to trust the natives on Bougainville despite the fact that there were coastwatchers there for intelligence purposes. The Solomon Islands natives were Christians. The Roman Catholic Church had a mission on the opposite side of the island and we were sent with mail-drops for them on many occasions. One of the most incongruous sights I ever saw was a Catholic nun in her flowing black and white gown riding in a jeep on the way to get on one of the airplanes to be evacuated. The Seventh Day Adventists had a mission in the New Georgia group. Sperzel returned from a search and reported that he had strafed a coastwise schooner in the New Georgia group, thinking that it was Japanese, and broke out crying when he found out that it belonged to the missionaries. It was embarrassing for him later to find out that he missed it completely.

Felix Cecot (Cisco) was of Polish extraction and a devout Roman Catholic. Whenever we had a particularly difficult flight, he would go to the priest for his confessions. When some of the natives came through our camp one afternoon, he asked the chief how many wives he had. The chief immediately began quoting Scripture to the effect that a man shall have only one wife, and continued with Scripture so that it was obvious that he knew more about the Bible than most of us. I would hope that our civilization has not done to these fine people what we have done in many other parts of the world, particularly to the natives of the Marshall Islands where I served my next tour of duty overseas.

The real souvenirs of the war were, in order, a samurai sword, a Japanese officer's pistol, and a flag. We were too far from the action on the front lines to be able to get any of these, but Ernie Brenner, our supply officer, was a past master at trading. When we came back from a long or difficult flight, the intelligence officer always gave us a two-ounce miniature of brandy. It was foul tasting and none of us ever drank it, but over time we each accumulated several bottles.

Everything we ate was dried—eggs, potatoes, lemonade, and everything you can imagine. One day after things had calmed down, Ernie said that he was going to go to the front lines and would take our brandy and try to trade it for some souvenirs. When he came back, he was loaded—flags, a pistol, and a sword. He had struck a gold mine and when we asked how he was able to trade the brandy for all of these souvenirs, he said that he had told the ground troopers that the brandy was dehydrated whiskey and that it was made for a canteen of water and when poured in the canteen it would be like a quart of whiskey. We suggested that he never go near the front lines again because they would use him for bait.

Russ Janson was one of the pilots with the most time in an SBD when we left the States. He probably had thirty-five hours. Russ was an engineering graduate of the University of Illinois where he received a commission in the Army. Prior to receiving the Army commission, he had tried to transfer to the Army Air Corps, and when they turned him down, he applied to the Navy for flight training and was a cadet when the commission came through. His

Russ Janson at our Guadalcanal tent with its surrounding jungle.

commission was revoked and so instead of building airfields, he was in the business of destroying them. As with most of us, he was a product of the Depression and had put himself through college by working—but Russ's job was anything but ordinary. He managed a sorority house and as a part of his remuneration, he lived there.

In the early mornings he was like an old bear, but after the initial shock of waking, he was the best company you could want, and could be counted on to carry more than his share of the load. Russ led the second division in the half of the squadron I led. He should have been the flight leader, but like Hap, he was lazy and did not want the responsibility of briefing and leading the hop. After Stock landed at Rennell and Jug was shot down, Russ was made to lead the other half. He wrote in his diary that he did not like it because of his responsibility for all of the planes on the flight, the TBFs and the fighters, and he hoped that he would not cause any of them to be killed. The SBDs were always the lead planes, and it was the flight leader's responsibility to keep everyone out of the clouds and to make the approach so that everyone was in the correct position for the attack.

Russ was the fastidious one of us. He hated dirt or mud in any form. When the shell from the cruiser failed to explode, and it was necessary for us to move our tents to the other side of the ridge, Russ decided that he did not want to get in the old, muddy, bug-infested foxholes in the middle of the night, and since there were only three of us, he dug a foxhole in our tent and lined it with blankets big enough for all three. Now when Washing Machine Charlie came over, he, Chuck Kollman, and I could all get in the hole without all of the inconvenience of the normal ones.

At about 11:00 A.M. on August 25, 1943, we were told that we were to be at operations at 12:00 to be ready to go home. Some of the others who had not yet been sent to Sydney for the third time had already left on a freighter. We were transported to the bomber strip and taken to the U.S.S. *Suwanee,* a small carrier. The trip back was a sheer pleasure. The food and living conditions were outstanding. We had no duties. We arrived at San Francisco and were driven to a troop train for transportation to the Naval Air Station at Miramar, just inland from San Diego. I was the senior officer and consequently was in charge of the troops. We had brought back with us the enlisted personnel from VMSB-141. The trip from San Francisco to Miramar took three days. We were sidetracked for every train we met.

I had a roster of the personnel I was accountable for. At the first roll call everyone answered, but a head count showed one person missing. I did everything possible, but there was no way to find out who the missing person was. Every time the train stopped, I had the roll called and a head count, without any solution. We finally arrived at NAS Miramar at 2:00 A.M. and lined up alongside the train. Another roll was called and head count was made, and everyone was there. I have never found out who the missing one was or how he found out when we were to arrive so that he could be there at the proper time.

One of my detail was a master sergeant who was being sent home for a general court-martial. He obviously was an old timer, and was being court-martialed for getting drunk and tearing up the officers' club at wing headquarters. On the carrier he was kept in the brig and I had no responsibility for him. On the train, I put him in one of the rooms and stationed guards with rifles on a twenty-four-hour basis. Our last stop before Miramar was Los Angeles. The conductor told me that we would be there for about six hours, and I gave all of the men liberty to do what they wished. The prisoner was guarded by two of the men. In walking through the railroad station, I came upon the prisoner sitting on one of the benches, holding the two rifles. I went over and asked the sergeant what was going on. He said, "Captain, neither of these two youngsters had ever been to Los Angeles and I told them that I would take care of these weapons and that I would be here when they came back. I have twenty years in the Marine Corps and intend to stay in. This court-martial isn't going to give me a discharge, so don't worry about me." I told him to take care of the rifles and went on about my business.

At NAS Miramar we were given thirty days' leave and ordered to report back to the west coast. Train travel was slow and uncertain. All of us, that is, Russ Janson, John Skinner, Felix Cecot, Hap Simpson, and I went downtown to inquire about commercial flights home. We went to the hotel in San Diego to the office of one of the airlines where we were told that in order to fly we must have a priority. The young lady working at the airline desk was as pretty as you could imagine and Russ asked her to have lunch with us. She accepted. At lunch she was questioned closely regarding priorities and how they were obtained. She said that it was only necessary for the commanding officer to fill out a form requesting the class priority that was necessary. Russ then ascertained what class was necessary to get through to our destination and, finally, where we could get the forms to request the priority. It turned out that she had the forms and would be glad to give them to us. All of them descended on me. I was their commanding officer. I could give them their priorities. This was not so, since any authority I had had terminated when we reached NAS Miramar, but I signed all of theirs, giving them a high enough priority so that they would not be put off the plane before they reached home. Now, what was *I* to do? Russ again solved the problem. A Marine on leave was his own commanding officer (according to Russ), and I, therefore, could sign my own. He never explained why that same logic did not apply to them.

On the way home, a Navy commander from Bessemer, executive officer of one of the carriers who had come back with us, was on the same plane with me. He was obviously a much more important personage than I. When we landed in Dallas, they told him they were sorry but he would have to get off the plane and wait for another as the other passengers had higher priorities. When I arrived in Birmingham, the mayor and other city officials from Bessemer were waiting to welcome him, and I had to tell them that he would be on a later plane. My mother and father were greatly impressed with my importance. I very obviously did not tell them why.

★ 12 ★

Reflections

Of the original pilots, Kelly, Kellogg, Kollman, Janson, Herlihy, Simpson, and Skinner each took regular commissions after the war. Cecot, Sperzel, and I went on inactive duty. Wallof was injured during the latter part of the war and was placed on retirement. Robertshaw was a regular officer and continued to retirement after serving as a lieutenant general. For the activities of the first tour, the various pilots were awarded two Navy Crosses, seven Distinguished Flying Crosses, and seven Air Medals. These awards were not based upon the number of combat missions flown but were for heroism and extraordinary achievement or for meritorious achievement against the enemy forces. Stock, Sperzel, Roberts, and I commanded squadrons later in the war.

In my opinion, they were the finest group of men I have ever known. They went into combat as young men, poorly trained and poorly equipped, met the enemy on its own terms, and through superb leadership, determination, patriotism, and guts were able to defeat the best that could be thrown at them. The November battle was the turning point of the war in the Pacific. Surely, it was not as spectacular as the victory at Midway, and certainly it did not receive the publicity of Midway; it nevertheless stopped the Japanese offensive. It is worthy of repetition that after this battle the enemy never went on the offensive again.

The officers, men, and pilots of VMSB-132 were a cross-section of America, from every region, from various backgrounds, but when the time came for them to be counted, they gave an account for which they, our country, their friends, and their families could well take pride. Their heritage, their education, and their family training combined to make them recognize their duty to their country and meet the challenge that was presented to them.

I am proud to have served with them.

Appendix 1

Medical Report of Flying Personnel of VMSB-132

MEDICAL DEPARTMENT
VMSB-132, MAG-11
C/O FLEET POST OFFICE
SAN FRANCISCO, CALIFORNIA

February 16, 1943

*REPORT ON FLYING PERSONNEL OF VMSB-132**

I joined VMSB-132 on September 28, 1942. We were in the States only until October 15, during which time all health records were brought up to date, including typhoid, tetanus, yellow fever, and smallpox vaccinations.

We arrived in Noumea October 29 with the squadron in good condition. Camp was established there for group-11. On the first of November four pilots were sent to Cactus with their gunners. Two of these pilots were lost on their first flight, one later proven dead, 2d Lt. W. R. Gentry, and the other carried as missing, 2d Lt. M. R. Nawman.

On the seventh of November nine pilots flew SBD-3s to Cactus, and on the fifteenth of November eight more pilots with gunners were flown up. The entire squadron was brought up via boat to Cactus on November 26 with one pilot, Capt. W. F. Spang, in command.

Capt. W. F. Spang was killed on an operational flight, his first night hop with a 1,000-pound bomb.

There were three more pilots and gunners lost during our stay: Maj. Joe Sailer, Jr., 2d Lt. F. L. Christian and 2d

* The text has been edited for consistency.

Lt. J. K. Rohrl. Major Sailer was seen to go into the water on his back after a Zero float plane had made two passes on him. His flaps had remained open after his dive. Second Lieutenant J. K. Rohrl never pulled out of his dive. Second Lieutenant F. L. Christian was lost in bad weather returning from an attack.

There were five medical evacuations:

(1) 2d Lt. A. B. Marvel after roughly forty hours flying time and four weeks in Cactus for malaria and "fear of the dark." To Cub Hospital.
(2) 2d Lt. C. L. Bright for malaria to Aviatorium.
(3) 2d Lt. H. C. Ball for malaria to Aviatorium.
(4) 2d Lt. P. H. Kellogg to Cub Hospital following crash with following injuries: Third degree burns of right arm and chest and lacerations of face and forehead.
(5) T. Sgt. B. L. Williams for malaria and chronic bronchitis and asthmatic breathing nightly. To Aviatorium.

Sixteen pilots were ordered out of Cactus December 24 with an average weight loss of fifteen pounds per man. The pilots after the fifth week showed definite signs of loss of efficiency and beginning carelessness. The food conditions were bad because of lack of food supplies and lack of cooking equipment.

Malaria was a problem in spite of constant prophylaxis with atabrine. Six of the pilots had positive smears upon arrival in Buttons. These were given thirty grains quinine daily for seven days while the rest of the pilots were flown to Australia for one week's leave. The balance of the pilots then went down with me to Australia after treatment.

After return from Australia 2d Lt. W. A. Eck and 2d Lt. W. H. Hronek were killed in operational accidents here at the "fighter strip." 2d Lt. W. H. Hronek was declared dead and 2d Lt. W. A. Eck missing.

The squadron has reclaimed three pilots who were evacuated to the Aviatorium. T. Sgt. B. L. Williams had to be sent to Cub Hospital with diagnosis of asthma two days after he returned. He was very much improved during his four weeks in the Aviatorium and one week in Australia but his asthma returned when he returned to the squadron. Second Lt. H. C. Ball and 2d Lt. C. L. Bright have returned to active duty with the squadron.

Constant atabrine prophylaxis is necessary for all men to prevent recurrences. The squadron has been swelled with transfers to a pilot strength of thirty. One pilot with malaria is at present in the group sick bay.

Seven cases of malaria among pilots at Cactus and four of the six positive smears after departure from Cactus had never had clinical symptoms of malaria. Thus eleven men out of twenty-seven had malaria in spite of atabrine prophylaxis of a minimum of four tablets a week.

R. J. JOHNSON,
Lt. (MC) U.S.N.R.

Appendix 2

Medical Report on Individual Pilots of VMSB-132

MEDICAL DEPARTMENT
HEADQUARTERS SQUADRON,
MARINE AIRCRAFT GROUP ELEVEN, F.M.F.
C/O FLEET POST OFFICE, SAN FRANCISCO, CALIFORNIA

February 22, 1943

FROM:	The Medical Officer, VMSB-132
TO:	The Wing Medical Officer, First Marine Aircraft Wing, F.M.F.
SUBJECT:	Report on each pilot individually.

1. 2d Lt. KELLY, R. E. entered combat 11-1-42 and was relieved 12-24-42. He had 65 hours combat, 25 missions, 6 attacks on ships, 3 hits. Good tolerance to combat. Malaria while in Cactus and positive smear upon arrival at Buttons. Seven days in Australia, and future flight status good.

2. 1st Lt. SPERZEL, J. E. (Executive Officer). Entered combat 11-7-42 and was relieved 12-24-42. He had 55 combat hours, 16 missions, 5 attacks on ships with 3 hits. Good tolerance to combat, malaria while in Cactus. Negative smear upon arrival at Buttons. Seven days in Australia with a future flight status that is good.

3. Major ROBERTSHAW, L. B. (Commanding Officer). Arrived Cactus 11-7-43, left 12-24-42, with 85 combat hours, 30 missions, and 6 attacks on ships with one hit. Excellent tolerance to combat, no disease or injury. Seven days in Australia. Negative malaria smears and future flight status excellent.

4. 2d Lt. McBRYDE, E. P. arrived combat 11-20-42 and left 12-24-42 with 35 hours combat, 13 missions, 4 attacks on ships and one hit. Good tolerance, no sickness or injury. Seven days in Australia. Positive malaria smear upon arrival in Buttons from Cactus. Future flight status good.

5. 1st Lt. McENIRY, J. H. to Cactus 11-7-42 and left 12-24-42, with 100 combat hours, 34 missions, 13 attacks and 4 hits on ships. Excellent tolerance to combat, no sickness or injury. Seven days in Australia, negative malaria smears, future flight status excellent.

6. 1st Lt. JACKSON, P. A. from 11-14-42 to 12-24-42 in Cactus. 70 combat hours, 23 missions, 8 attacks, and 5 hits. Good tolerance to combat, positive smear upon arrival in Buttons from Cactus, no sickness. Small shrapnel wound in left thigh 12-23-42. Seven days in Australia, and future flight status good.

7. 1st Lt. HERLIHY, G. B. arrived 11-7-42 and left 12-24-42, 110 hours combat, 33 missions, 5 attacks on ships with 4 hits. Excellent tolerance to combat, no sickness, compound dislocation of right thumb 12-10-42. No flying for seven days, negative malaria smears. Seven days in Australia, future flight status excellent.

8. 2d Lt. SIMPSON, A. D. arrived 11-7-42 left Cactus 12-24-42, 100 combat hours, 11 attacks, 3 hits. Good tolerance to combat, negative malaria smears. Seven days in Australia, no illness or injury. Excellent future flight status.

9. 1st Lt. CECOT, F. S. arrived 11-14-42 left Cactus 12-24-42, 55 combat hours, 28 missions, 10 attacks, with 3 hits. Good tolerance to combat, negative malaria smears, no illness or injury. Seven days in Australia, good future flight status.

10. 2d Lt. SKINNER, J. Jr. arrived 11-8-42, left Cactus 12-24-42, 80 combat hours, 35 missions, 9 attacks, 3 hits. No illness or injury. Positive smear before Australia trip. Seven days in Australia. Good future flight status.

11. Mar. Gun. GORDON, K. D. arrived 11-7-42, left Cactus 12-24-42, 90 combat hours, 34 missions, 10 attacks,

and 2 hits. No illness or injury. Good tolerance to combat, negative malaria smears. Seven days in Australia, and good future flight status.

12. S. Sgt. WALLOF, E. J. arrived 11-7-42, left Cactus 12-24-42, 90 combat hours, 34 missions, 10 attacks, and 2 hits. No injury, dermatitis while in Cactus. Grounded for seven days. Good tolerance to combat, positive malaria smear upon arrival in Button from Cactus. Seven days in Australia, and good future flight status.

13. 1st Lt. JANSON, R. L. arrived 11-7-42, left Cactus 12-24-42, 93 combat hours, 6 attacks, 2 hits. No illness or injury. Good tolerance to combat, positive smear upon arrival Buttons from Cactus. Seven days in Australia, good future flight status.

14. Maj. SAILER, J. Jr. arrived 11-1-42, reported missing in action 12-7-42. 50 combat hours, 13 attacks on ships with 9 hits.

15. Capt. SPANG, W. F. arrived 11-26-42 and killed in action 12-1-42 with 6 combat hours and 2 missions.

16. 1st Lt. BALL, H. C. arrived 11-7-42, left Cactus 12-12-42, 50 combat hours, 21 missions, 4 attacks and no hits. Poor tolerance to combat; he had malaria and had a wisdom tooth pulled during stay at Cactus. Evacuated to Aviatorium 12-12-42. There had negative smear and remained there 5 weeks. Seven days in Australia, very poor future flight status. It is my belief that 1st Lt. Ball is flying purely for flight pay and the easiest way he can get it the better. He is entirely untrustworthy when the going gets rough and cares only for his own personal well being.

17. 1st Lt. BRIGHT, C. L. arrived 11-6-42, to Aviatorium, 51.7 hours combat, 30 missions, 7 attacks, and 0 hits. Malaria, but no injuries while in Cactus. Good tolerance to combat, negative malaria smears at Aviatorium, at Aviatorium 5 weeks, then one week in Australia. Future flight status good. Rejoined squadron 1-27-43.

18. 1st Lt. KOLLMAN, C. E. arrived 11-7-42, left Cactus 12-24-42. 60 combat hours, 26 missions, 6 attacks, 4 hits.

Good tolerance to combat, malaria twice in Cactus. Seven days in Australia, excellent future flight status.

19. 2d Lt. KELLOGG, P. H. arrived 11-15-42, left Cactus 12-14-42, 25 combat hours, 10 missions, 1 attack, no hits. He crashed on take-off 12-13-42 resulting with 3rd degree burns on right arm and right chest. Evacuated 12-14-42 to Cub #1 Hospital. From there to Solace. Good tolerance to combat. Future flight status questionable. Severe diarrhea while in Cactus for 10 days.

20. 1st Lt. ROHRL, J. K. arrived 11-15-42, mission [*sic*] in action 12-11-42. 20 combat hours, 6 missions and one attack from which he never returned. Good tolerance to combat. No illness or injuries previous to reported missing.

21. S. Sgt. WILLIAMS, B. L. arrived 11-15-42, left Cactus 12-14-42, 30 combat hours, 11 missions, and no attacks. Malaria, chronic bronchitis and bronchial asthma. Evacuated to Aviatorium 12-14-42, there 5 weeks, then seven days in Australia, reported in to squadron 1-27-43 and on 1-30-43 evacuated to Cub Hospital with return of asthma, from there to Solace. Good tolerance to combat and future flying status good with climatic change.

22. 2d Lt. CHRISTIAN, F. L. arrived 11-15-42, reported missing 12-16-42. 60 combat hours, 22 missions, 3 attacks, no hits, did not return from last attack. Good tolerance to combat. No injury or illness.

23. 1st Lt. ECK, W. A. arrived 11-5-42, left Cactus 12-24-42, 110 hours, 44 missions, 12 attacks, 3 hits. Good tolerance to combat, no illness or injuries. No malaria and excellent future flight status. Seven days in Australia, killed 1-21-43 in operations from fighter strip here at Buttons. Reported missing.

24. 1st Lt. HRONEK, W. H. arrived 11-5-42, left Cactus 12-24-42, 70 combat hours, 33 missions, 8 attacks, 0 hits. No malaria or injuries. Grounded 5 days with boil of right thigh. Good tolerance to combat, future flight status good. Seven days in Australia, killed in operational flight 1-23-43 at fighter strip in Buttons.

25. 2d Lt. NAWMAN, M. R., arrived 11-1-42, reported missing in action on first flight 11-2-42 at Cactus.

26. 2d Lt. GENTRY, W. R. arrived 11-1-42 and killed in action 11-2-42 at Cactus.

27. 2d Lt. HERRICK, D. L. arrived 11-16-42, left Cactus 12-29-42, 50 combat hours, 13 missions, 4 attacks, one hit. Wounded in action 12-22-42, shrapnel wound of right leg, grounded seven days. Good tolerance to combat, malaria in Cactus. Seven days in Australia. Returned to squadron and transferred to VMSB-234 approximately 2-1-43. Future flight status good.

28. 2d Lt. MARVEL, A. B. arrived 11-15-42, left Cactus 12-1-42, 30 combat hours, 11 missions, 2 attacks, 0 hits. Poor tolerance to combat, evacuated to Cub, but instead of there he ended up in some Army Hospital. Address unknown to this date because of fear of the dark. Future flight status questionable in combat zone. No illness or injury.

The following named officers joined squadron VMSB-132 January 21, 1943:

McARDLE, R. H.	2d Lt.
DIEFFENBACH, K. H.	2d Lt.
BLAINE, R.	2d Lt.
ROBERTS, T. R.	1st Lt.
POPE, F. C. Jr.	2d Lt.
McALLISTER, J. G.	2d Lt.

The following named officers and men joined VMSB-132 from VMSB-142 February 4, 1943, and my knowledge of them is meager. They are at present, with the exception of McDERMOTT, F.G., in Australia for seven days.

29. McDERMOTT, F. G., 2d Lt. arrived 1-4-43, left Cactus 1-20-43. 15 combat hours, no attacks. Good tolerance, no illness and future flight status good.

30. McGUCKIN, J., 1st Lt. in Cactus approximately 3 weeks, left 1-26-43. Good tolerance, no illness.

31. STOCK, J. H., 1st Lt. in Cactus approximately 3 weeks, left 1-26-43. Good tolerance, no illness.

32. HICKS, H. H., T. Sgt. arrived 11-16-42, left Cactus

1-24-43. Approximately 80 hours. Good tolerance, future flight status good. No illness or injury.

33. BENECHE, A. C., T. Sgt. arrived 11-11-42, left Cactus 11-22-42. Arrived Cactus 12-15-42, left Cactus 1-26-43. Approximately 80 hours. Good tolerance and good future flight status. No illness or injury.

34. MINOR, R. D., T. Sgt. No combat hours. He had malaria 3 times here at Buttons.

35. HUMPHREY, E. H., T. Sgt. Flight orders revoked by Wing General Order and he was sent to classification center at Noumea. This due to Humphrey's desire to be grounded.

/S/ R. J. Johnson

Appendix 3

Personnel of VMSB-132 Killed or Missing in Action and Presumed Dead during Its Tours of Duty at Guadalcanal, 1942–1943

NAME	RANK	DATE
Christian, Frank L. (pilot)	2d Lt.	Dec. 16, 1942
Eck, Walter A. (pilot)	1st Lt.	Jan. 21, 1943
Gentry, Wayne R. (pilot)	2d Lt.	Nov. 2, 1942
Gordon, Kenneth D. (pilot)	WO	June 2, 1943
Hronek, William H., Jr. (pilot)	2d Lt.	Jan. 23, 1943
Jackson, Andrew (pilot)	Capt.	June 9, 1943
McArdle, Robert H. (pilot)	Capt.	June 30, 1943
Nawman, Melvin R. (pilot)	2d Lt.	Nov. 2, 1942
Rohrl, Joseph K. (pilot)	1st Lt.	Dec. 11, 1942
Sailer, Joseph, Jr. (pilot)	Maj.	Dec. 7, 1942
Spang, William F. (pilot)	Capt.	Dec. 1, 1942
Hicks, Howard R. (pilot)	M. Sgt.	June 2, 1943
Irons, Albert R. (gunner)	Pfc.	June 30, 1943
Korotki, Irvin P. (gunner)	Pfc.	Jan. 21, 1943
Lagtola, Vilo P. (gunner)	Pvt.	Nov. 2, 1942
Quinn, Thomas, Jr. (gunner)	S. Sgt.	June 9, 1943
Shattuck, Glenn (gunner)	Pfc.	Dec. 16, 1942
Wellington, Francis G. (gunner)	Cpl.	Dec. 11, 1943
Wilhelm, Gerhart (gunner)	Cpl.	Nov. 2, 1942

Bibliography

Coggins, Jack. *The Campaign for Guadalcanal.* New York: Doubleday & Co., 1972.

DeChant, John A. *Devilbirds.* New York: Harper and Brothers, 1947.

Hoyt, Edwin P. *Guadalcanal.* New York: Steire and Day, 1982.

Hubler, Richard G., and DeChant, John A. *Flying Leathernecks.* New York: Doubleday, Doran & Co., 1944.

Lee, Robert Edward. *Victory at Guadalcanal.* Novato, Calif.: Presidio Press, 1981.

Manchester, William. *Goodbye Darkness.* Boston: Little, Brown & Co., 1980.

Merillat, Herbert C. *Guadalcanal Revisited.* New York: Dodd, Mead & Co., 1982.

Merillat, H. C. *The Island, A History of the Marines on Guadalcanal.* Boston: Houghton Mifflin Co., 1944.

Miller, Thomas G. *The Cactus Air Force.* New York: Harper & Row, 1969.

Morison, Samuel E. *History of United States Naval Operations in World War II,* Vol. V, *The Struggle for Guadalcanal.* New York: Little, Brown & Co., 1949.

Sherrod, Robert. *History of Marine Corps Aviation in World War II.* Washington: Cambat Forces Press, 1952.

Tanaka, Razio. *Japan's Losing Struggle for Guadalcanal.* Annapolis, Md.: United States Naval Institute Proceedings, August 1956.

Tillman, Barrett. *The Dauntless Dive Bomber of World War Two.* Annapolis, Md.: United States Naval Institute Press, 1976.

Toland, John. *The Rising Sun.* New York: Random House, 1970.

Wilcox, Roger. *Unaccustomed To Fear: Biography of the Late General Roy S. Geiger USMC*. Privately Published, 1968.

Wolfert, Ira. "A Grandstand View of Jap Naval Disaster." *Reader's Digest,* February 1943 (Condensed from *New York Times*).

Index

Lt. J. H. McEniry, awarded DFC for action at Guadalcanal on first tour.

About the Author

COLONEL JOHN HOWARD MCENIRY, JR. USMCR Ret. practiced law in Bessemer, Alabama until his retirement in 1982. He received his B.A. and LL.B. degrees from The University of Alabama. He served in the U.S. Marine Corps as a dive-bomber pilot at Guadalcanal in 1942–1943 and subsequently as a commanding officer of a fighter bomber squadron in the Central Pacific. At the conclusion of World War II he was serving in headquarters U.S. Marine Corps in Washington, D.C. He was awarded seven Distinguished Flying Crosses, eighteen Air Medals, Presidential Unit Citation, and seven battle stars on the South Pacific Ribbon.

After the war he was the commanding officer of the Marine Reserve Squadron and the Marine Reserve Air Group at Birmingham. He was recalled for the Korean War and served as the commanding officer of the Attack Training Squadron at the MCAS Cherry Point, North Carolina.